HOW TO PLAN THE
PERFECT GARDEN

GARDEN *KNOW-HOW*

HOW TO PLAN THE
PERFECT GARDEN

PETER McHOY

southwater

6/04

This edition is published by Southwater

Southwater is an imprint of Anness Publishing Ltd
Hermes House, 88–89 Blackfriars Road, London SE1 8HA
tel. 020 7401 2077; fax 020 7633 9499
www.southwaterbooks.com; info@anness.com

© Anness Publishing Ltd 1996, 2003

UK agent: The Manning Partnership Ltd,
6 The Old Dairy, Melcombe Road, Bath BA2 3LR;
tel. 01225 478444; fax 01225 478440; sales@manning-partnership.co.uk

UK distributor: Grantham Book Services Ltd,
Isaac Newton Way, Alma Park Industrial Estate, Grantham, Lincs NG31 9SD;
tel. 01476 541080; fax 01476 541061; orders@gbs.tbs-ltd.co.uk

North American agent/distributor: National Book Network,
4501 Forbes Boulevard, Suite 200, Lanham, MD 20706;
tel. 301 459 3366; fax 301 429 5746; www.nbnbooks.com

Australian agent/distributor: Pan Macmillan Australia,
Level 18, St Martins Tower, 31 Market St, Sydney, NSW 2000;
tel. 1300 135 113; fax 1300 135 103; customer.service@macmillan.com.au

New Zealand agent/distributor: David Bateman Ltd,
30 Tarndale Grove, Off Bush Road, Albany, Auckland;
tel. (09) 415 7664; fax (09) 415 8892

A CIP catalogue record for this book is
available from the British Library.

Publisher: Joanna Lorenz
Senior Editor: Lindsay Porter
Designer: Lilian Lindblom
Illustrator: Michael Shoebridge
Photography credits see page 96

Previously published as
*Practical Gardening Library:
Plan a Perfect Garden*

1 3 5 7 9 10 8 6 4 2

CONTENTS

Introduction	6
PRINCIPLES OF DESIGN AND PLANNING	8
GARDEN IDEAS	26
THE GOOD PLANT GUIDE	84
Index	95
Acknowledgements	96

INTRODUCTION

Improving your garden, giving it individuality, is surprisingly easy – if you take a step-by-step approach. Garden improvements are often physically demanding, but you can choose a design that keeps heavy construction to the minimum. Producing a creative design can be difficult if you start with a blank sheet of paper and no inspiration, but you will not have that problem with this book by your side.

You cannot build a successful garden by following "recipes" or copying someone else's design exactly, however. Gardens are different: sizes and shapes vary enormously, and plants that may thrive in one garden may be unsuitable for the soil or aspect in another. Your garden is unlikely to be identical to one for which a plan in a book or magazine was drawn. In your own garden, the patio may end up in the shade instead of the sun, and plants for a shady wall might be positioned against a sunny one.

So use the ideas in this book for inspiration, and adapt them to suit your own preferences, budget and available time. Do not be afraid to take an idea from one garden and work it into the plan for another. Above all, do not be put off by the prospect of redesigning your garden. It can be fun in the planning and enormously rewarding in the execution and construction. You will also achieve a garden that reflects your individual personality and taste, and have the satisfaction that you have created something special.

Gardening is something more than a collection of plants in beds and borders – it is about creating an overall effect, a statement of your idea of a good garden, in which the plants and the hard landscaping (paving and walls, for example) both play a vital part.

Problems in perspective

If you tackle a garden in sections, the improvements will seem much more achievable, be easier on the purse or wallet, and take less effort to attain. This is true even for a small garden.

By all means have an overall scheme in mind and roughed out on paper if the garden is large, but work in detail on just one section of the garden at a time. Tackle the front garden, or the back garden, or perhaps just the patio, and construct that before moving on to the next task, which, perhaps, will wait for next year. In this way you see the improvements quickly without the garden construction becoming a chore.

The illustrations on these two pages are the story of how one small garden was improved in stages. They show how various parts of this small garden have been treated in different styles, each tackled as a separate project each year.

1 To reduce the maintenance involved in a narrow flowerbed, it was transformed into a "stream" and bog garden, using a long and narrow liner (you will have to order a non-standard size like this). This took a couple of weekends to finish, but added variety and attracted lots of wildlife.

2 The original paving slab path on a concrete base was left *in situ* to save the considerable effort of breaking it up. Instead, pieces of slate were simply mortared over the top of the old path, a job done in a day, so the transformation was almost instant. A pond was introduced to offset the potentially harsh outline of the conifers and gravel.

3 The back garden, which is equally small, was tackled the following year. Despite its size, it was divided into two sections, to introduce variety and to make the garden seem larger. This also had the added benefit of having one attractive area in the garden, while construction of the other half followed at a later date. The trellis acts as a partition without shutting out too much light.

4 This half of the back garden was constructed later, using a different type of paving and with more extensive use of compact shrubs planted directly into the soil, thus creating a different atmosphere from the rest of the garden.

5 It makes sense to start with the front garden as this is what passers-by and visitors see first. This small front garden was originally lawn with a narrow flowerbed on the other side of a boring path of rectangular paving slabs. It was transformed into an attractive low-maintenance garden in a couple of weekends by digging up the grass and planting slow-growing conifers with contrasting shapes and colours. The area between them was covered with gravel to suppress weeds.

Principles of design

With a few exceptions – such as wild gardens or those with an informal country cottage style, for example – the hallmark of a well-designed garden is that it has either a strong theme or detectable pattern. If your interest lies primarily in plants; clever planting patterns, or pretty colour themes, or contrast, these will be enough to give your garden that special look. Usually, however, it is the hard landscaping that gives a garden a strong sense of having been designed.

One way to guarantee impact in a small area is to mix paving materials and introduce small changes in level.

The design here has a strongly rectangular theme, but because of the variety of textures and changes of level, it doesn't look boring.

This professionally designed garden also shows the importance of foliage plants and the role of moving water as a focal point.

This combination of both a creative use of plants and strong hard landscaping has the indisputable hallmark of careful planning and design. Even in a small area like this, the impact is immediate.

Circular themes can be difficult to accommodate in a small garden, and where the circles leave awkward angles, they can be hard to manage. Here the problem has been overcome by the clever use of water, with bold plants to help mask transition points.

The choice of a single specimen plant with an almost spherical outline, off-set to one side of the decking, combines simplicity with good taste and a strong sense of design. Garden size is less important than how you use the space.

As a basic shape, gardens cannot be any simpler than this, but even a quick glance tells you that it has the stamp of a very experienced designer. The plants in this country garden have that magical cottage garden look, yet they have been framed in a clearly modern setting.

Bricks and clay pavers are an excellent choice for this kind of informal planting as they have a mellowness that complements the plants. This very simple design works so well because the pavers have been laid in an interesting herringbone pattern with a crisp outline around the inner bed.

Focal points are very important, and even a potentially dull or boring corner of the garden can be transformed into an area of special charm with the imaginative use of a focal point. Before a focal point was introduced, this small path led between some shrubs to the boundary hedge, and was a very dull part of the garden that you would not want to show your visitors. A couple of slate steps and a Japanese lantern set in a small gravelled area were all that was needed to transform this area into a feature that seldom fails to attract favourable comment.

Improving your garden does not necessarily mean a major redesign. Often, only small changes or the clever use of focal points are all that is required.

Left: *Multiple and linking circles always make a better design than individual or isolated circular areas. This design is particularly effective because the circular pond is reflected in the edging, the band of grass, and then the surrounding brick path, rather like ripples in a pool. By using the same bricks for the path leading to this part of the garden, the whole feature has been well integrated.*

Above: *If you take over a mature garden, with large trees and shrubs, you may feel that major reconstruction would be too demanding. Often, however, a few simple modifications will achieve a transformation.*

The addition of a couple of formal beds edged with box is sufficient to transform a plain lawn into something more formal that seems appropriate for this style of older garden. But it still needs colour and a central focal point to create a sense of design, and here it has been achieved with a large and attractively planted urn.

To give your garden a strong appeal, it is not necessary to destroy most of what is there already. Sometimes it is sufficient to remove one or two features and perhaps create an area of strong visual appeal in their place.

Deciding on priorities

It makes sense to begin any garden design by making a wish-list. It is most unlikely to be fulfilled completely, but setting down those things that are a priority to you should ensure that the most important features are included.

MAKING YOUR LIST

Everyone has different preferences, so make a list like the one shown here (photocopy it if you don't want to write your own or mark the book). Decide which features you regard as essential (this may be something as mundane as a clothes drier or as interesting as a water feature), those that are important but less essential for your ideal garden, and those elements that you regard simply as desirable. While designing your garden, keep in mind those features listed as essential. Try to incorporate as many of them as possible, but don't cram in so many that the strong sense of design is sacrificed.

It will immediately become apparent if the list of the most desirable features is not feasible within the limited space available, but you will probably be able to introduce some of the more important ones. However, only attempt to include those features ticked as desirable if you have space.

Working from a check-list will not directly aid the design, but it will act as a reminder of what is important to you. A garden that fulfils the functions that are important may be more satisfying than one that is well designed and smart but omits features that you care about.

GARDEN PRIORITIES

	Essential	Important	Desirable
Flowerbeds	[ ]	[ ]	[ ]
Herbaceous border	[ ]	[ ]	[ ]
Shrub border	[ ]	[ ]	[ ]
Trees	[ ]	[ ]	[ ]
Lawn	[ ]	[ ]	[ ]
Gravelled area	[ ]	[ ]	[ ]
Paved area/patio	[ ]	[ ]	[ ]
Built-in barbecue	[ ]	[ ]	[ ]
Garden seats/furniture	[ ]	[ ]	[ ]
Rock garden	[ ]	[ ]	[ ]
Pond	[ ]	[ ]	[ ]
Other water feature	[ ]	[ ]	[ ]
Wildlife area	[ ]	[ ]	[ ]
Greenhouse/ conservatory	[ ]	[ ]	[ ]
Summerhouse	[ ]	[ ]	[ ]
Tool shed	[ ]	[ ]	[ ]
Fruit garden	[ ]	[ ]	[ ]
Herb garden	[ ]	[ ]	[ ]
Vegetable garden	[ ]	[ ]	[ ]
Trellis/ pergola/arch	[ ]	[ ]	[ ]
Sand pit/ play area	[ ]	[ ]	[ ]
Clothes drier/line	[ ]	[ ]	[ ]
Dustbin hide	[ ]	[ ]	[ ]
....	[ ]	[ ]	[ ]
....	[ ]	[ ]	[ ]
....	[ ]	[ ]	[ ]
....	[ ]	[ ]	[ ]
....	[ ]	[ ]	[ ]

Be flexible in your approach to features. If a pond is on your list but there does not seem to be sufficient space or an appropriate place to build it, consider a small patio pond like this one.

The tool shed is always difficult to accommodate, as it should not be obtrusive. With clever planting, however, it can usually be screened well enough to be acceptable.

A permanent barbecue may look impressive when entertaining, but bear in mind that it can also look bleak in winter. You may prefer a portable one that can be removed when it is not required.

Right: *If you want a pergola but there is not space for a free-standing one, a patio overhead that links house and garden could be a sensible alternative. Linking house and garden visually can be an important element in good garden design.*

Surveying and measuring

It is much better – and less expensive – to make your mistakes on paper first, so the starting point for any garden improvement plan should be to prepare a sketch and plan of the garden as it is. This can then be worked up into any number of imaginative designs, and if things do not work out as you expected, just rub it out or put it in the bin, and start again.

WHAT YOU WILL NEED

- A 30m (100ft) tape measure – preferably plasticized fabric as this is easy to work with, but does not stretch.
- A 1.8m (6ft) steel rule for short measurements.
- Pegs to mark out positions, and to hold one end of the tape in position (meat skewers can be used with the tape).
- Pencils, sharpener and eraser.
- Clipboard with pad or graph paper.

POSITIONING FEATURES

With a small rectangular garden, like the one shown here, most measurements are easily determined by measuring key points from a known straight line such as the house or a fence. If the shape is more complicated, it is usually possible to determine a position by laying a piece of string at right angles from the known straight edge, then measuring at right angles from this at a point marked on your sketch. This avoids the slightly more complicated method of positioning such as triangulation, described on page 17.

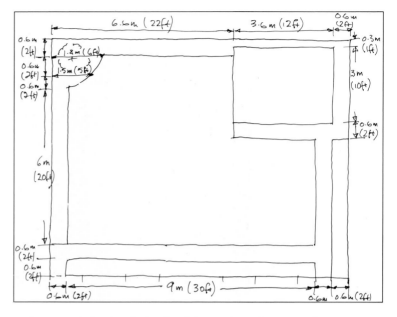

Make a rough freehand sketch of the garden. If it is very large, divide it into sections that can be pieced together later, but for a small garden like this, the whole area will go onto a single sheet of paper.

If necessary, join several sheets of paper together rather than cramp the sketch, and leave plenty of space around the edge on which you can write the dimensions.

Write down the measurements of all the main features, like paths, sheds and greenhouses, and important flowerbeds and large trees. Do not include anything that you are already sure you will not retain, otherwise include as many measurements as possible.

COPING WITH SLOPES

- Professional landscape architects surveying a large garden will use special techniques to determine the slope, which is then transferred to the plan as contour lines. However, most simple garden improvements can be achieved quite successfully without this degree of accuracy.

- If the slope is very gradual, you can ignore it, unless you want to create a deliberate change of level. More significant slopes can usually be estimated and the contours drawn in by eye. If the slope is steep, or if you want to create a series of terraces, you will have to measure the slope accurately and incorporate it into your scale drawing. Usually, however, it is possible to improve your garden simply by using the methods suggested in this book.

Gentle slopes over a short distance seldom present a problem. A couple of very shallow terraces that do not need strong retaining walls are usually sufficient to create plenty of level ground for a lawn, for example, and then the final steeper bank can be clothed with rock plants. These will look attractive, tolerate the dry conditions found on sloping ground and, once established, will help to stabilize the soil.

Putting the plan on paper

The exciting part of replanning your garden starts when you have an outline of the existing garden and permanent fixtures on which you can start to create your dream garden. It has all the excitement and promise of reading seed catalogues, where the imagination transforms the existing garden into an area full of beauty and promise. Making an accurate scale drawing of your existing garden is an essential starting point if you want to simplify the design work that follows.

QUICK ON THE DRAW

1 Draw the outline of the garden first, together with the position of the house and any other features, and make sure you have the correct measurements for these before filling in the other elements.

2 Next, draw in those elements that are easy to position, such as rectangular flowerbeds or raised beds and the garden shed, if you are reasonably certain of exactly where they are.

3 Ink in those elements of the garden that are fixed and will not change, such as boundaries and paths that you know you will not move. Draw the other parts in pencil first, as it is quite likely that you may have to make slight adjustments. Ink them in when you know everything is in its correct place.

4 Use a compass if possible to draw curves and circles. Not all curves are suitable for this treatment, but you can buy flexible rules that can be bent to any reasonable curve.

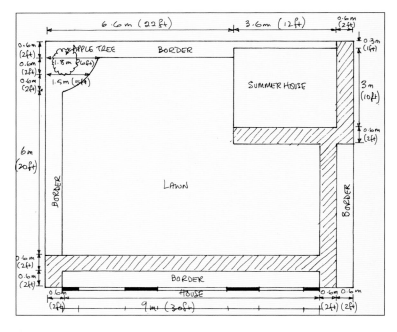

The rough sketch must be transferred to a scale drawing before any detailed plans can be sketched out. Drawing it to scale will help you in calculating the amount of any paving required, and also enable you to make beds, borders and lawns to sizes that involve the least amount of cutting of hard materials such as paving slabs or bricks.

Use graph paper for your scale drawing. Pads are adequate for a small garden or a section of a larger one, but if your garden is big, buy a large sheet (available from good stationers and art shops).

Use a scale that enables you to fit the plan onto your sheet of graph paper (or several taped together). For most small gardens, a scale of 1:50 (2cm to 1m or ¼in to 1ft) is about right. For a large garden, however, 1:100 (1cm to 1m or ⅛in to 1ft) might be more appropriate.

Draw the basic outline and the position of the house first, including the position of doors and windows if relevant. Then add all the major features that you are likely to retain. You should have all the necessary measurements on the freehand sketch that you made in the garden.

Omit any features that you are sure will be eliminated from the new design, to keep it as uncluttered as possible. In this example, the summerhouse has been drawn in because it was considered to be in a good position and would be difficult to move. The corner tree was removed in the final design, but was included at this stage as a design might have been chosen that made use of it.

USING YOUR PLAN

1 Even expert designers make a number of rough sketches of possible designs before finalizing the chosen one, so devise a way of using your master outline again and again without having to keep redrawing it. One way is to make a number of photocopies.

2 If you have a drawing board, simply use tracing paper overlays for your roughs while experimenting with ideas. If you do not have a drawing board and the garden is small, you may be able to use a clipboard instead.

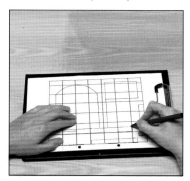

3 Film and pens of the type used for overhead projection sheets are effective if you prefer to use colours that can easily be wiped off for correction.

4 Some people prefer visual aids to move around when designing. If you find this helpful, try drawing and cutting out scale features that you want to include in your finished design, such as a raised pond, patio furniture, or raised beds. These can be moved around until they look right, but they should only be used as aids once the overall design has been formulated in your mind. If you try to design your garden around the few key symbols that you have placed, it will lack coherence.

DESIGNING BY COMPUTER

- If you feel happier with a computer keyboard and mouse than with paper and pencil, you can use one of the several computer programs that are available to help you design your garden.

- These vary enormously in capability and ease of use. The cheaper ones are likely to be fairly basic, and you may find them more frustrating to use than you imagine. The more sophisticated programs are both versatile and effective, but unless you intend to design gardens on a regular basis, they are probably not worth the money and time needed to learn how to use them properly.

- You will find pencil and paper just as effective for a one-off design for your own garden, with minimal financial outlay and the decided advantage of being able to move around your garden while modifying the plan.

TRIANGULATION MADE EASY

- Sometimes it may be difficult to measure a position simply by using right angles: perhaps there is an obstruction such as a pond or low hedge, for example, or there may be no available right angles because of the shape of the garden. Triangulation is a way of fixing a position, and is much easier than it sounds.

- Using known points, the corners of the house in this example, simply measure the distance to the position to be fixed, and note the two distances on your sketch.

- When you make your scale drawing, set a compass to each of the scale distances in turn, then strike an arc in the approximate position. The point you measured in the garden is where the arcs intersect on the plan.

To fix the position of the tree, measure to A, then B. Strike arcs on a scale drawing with compasses set at these measurements. The point where the arcs cross indicates the position of the tree in relation to the house.

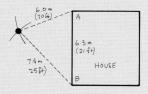

Creating your design

The difficult part of redesigning or improving your garden is making a start. After you start drawing, the ideas are sure to flow, especially if you have other gardens in mind that you like and can use as a starting point. The many inspirational pictures in this book will provide a wealth of ideas that you can adapt for your own garden, but take elements from various gardens that you like rather than try to recreate someone else's design exactly. Designs seldom transfer easily unless your garden is very similar in shape and size, and your garden will be much more satisfying if it reflects your own personality and preferences.

PLANNING THE SHAPE OF THE GARDEN

If you decide on a garden with strong lines, rather than irregular flowing borders, wildlife corners and semi-woodland areas, it is worth deciding on whether you are going to plan a rectangular or diagonal theme, or use a design based on circles. Any of these can be adapted to suit the size of your garden, and in the case of the circular pattern, you might want to include overlapping circles. Where circles join, try to make any transitional curves gradual rather than abrupt.

Whichever you choose, draw a grid on top of your plan to aid design (see opposite page). In a small garden surrounded by fencing, it can be useful to base the rectangular and diagonal grids on the spacing of fence posts (usually about 1.8m (6ft) apart).

A rectangular grid has been used for the example opposite, but as part of the trial-and-error phase, it is usually worth trying different grids. A diagonal grid is often particularly effective where the house is set in a large garden with plenty of space at the sides. The patio can often be positioned at a 45-degree angle at the corner of the house, for example.

The size and shape of the garden will usually dictate the most appropriate grid, but if in doubt, try more than one to see which one emerges with more possibilities than the others after a few attempts at quick designs.

Bear in mind that many excellent, prize-winning gardens are created without such a grid, and sometimes these have, to some extent, evolved in a more flowing manner, developing feature by feature. Grids like these may help you, but do not hesitate to adopt a more freestyle approach if this comes more naturally.

CIRCULAR THEME

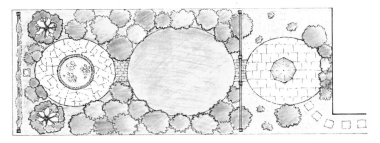

DIAGONAL THEME

RECTANGULAR THEME

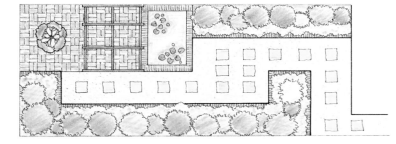

BEGINNING THE DESIGN

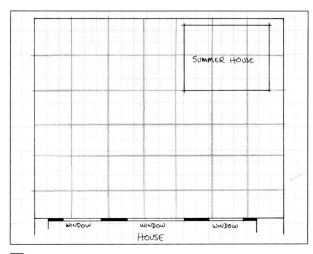

1 Draw in any features to be retained (in this example the summerhouse), and the chosen grid (unless you want an informal style where a grid may be inappropriate). Use a different colour for the grid lines, in order to prevent the plan becoming cluttered and confused.

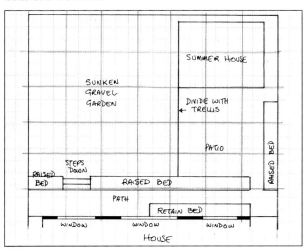

2 Use overlays (or photocopies) to experiment with a range of designs. Even if the first attempt looks satisfactory, try a number of variations. You can always come back to your first idea later if it turns out to be the best one.

At this stage, do not include details such as patio furniture or individual plants (except for key focal point plants and important trees or shrubs). When you have a design that you like, pencil in things like patio furniture (or use the cut-out features if you prepared them earlier).

TEN TIPS TO TRY

Don't despair if inspiration does not come easily, or initial attempts seem disappointing. If you try these ten tips, you will almost certainly produce workable plans that you will be pleased with:

- Look through books and magazines to decide which style of garden you like: formal or informal; the emphasis on plants or on hard landscaping; mainly foliage, texture and ground cover or lots of colourful flowers; straight edges or curved and flowing lines.

- With the style decided, look at as many garden pictures as possible – make a start in this book – and look for design ideas that appeal. Do not be influenced by individual plants, as these can be changed.

- Choose a grid, if applicable, as described on page 18, and draw this onto your plan. This will help to carry your thoughts through on logical lines.

- Start sketching lots of designs but do not attempt to perfect them at this stage. Just explore ideas.

- Do not concern yourself with planning plants or attempt to choose individual plants at this stage – concentrate on patterns and lines.

- Do not spend time drawing in paving patterns or choosing materials yet.

- Make a short list of those overall outlines that you like best. Then forget it for a day. It always pays to take a fresh look at things after a short break.

- If you still like one of your original roughs, begin to work on that, filling in details like paving, surface textures such as gravel, and the position of focal point plants, etc. Leave out planting plans at this stage.

- If your original roughs lack appeal when you look at them again, repeat the process with another batch of ideas. You will probably see ways of improving some of your earlier efforts, so things will be easier this time round.

- If you find it difficult to visualize sizes, peg the design out on the ground with string (see pages 20–21), and modify your plan if necessary.

Finishing touches

When the outline plan is ready, it's time to fill in the detail and to make sure it will work on the ground. Designs can look very different in actual size and when viewed three-dimensionally rather than as a flat plan on paper. This is the time for fine-tuning, for selecting paving materials, adjusting the plan to minimize the number of cut bricks or slabs, and for visualizing the changes on the ground.

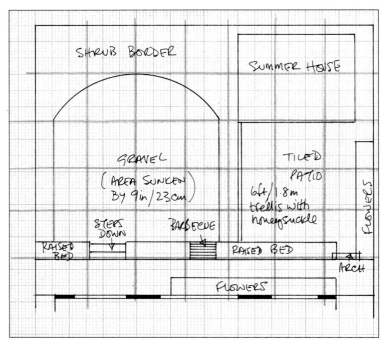

If your design includes irregularly shaped beds, use a length of hose-pipe or thick rope to mark out the shape. If you have to cut the beds into an existing lawn, you will need to do this anyway when it's time to start construction.

When the main features and their position have been decided, draw up a detailed plan, such as the one above. It will almost certainly be necessary to make some adjustments to the rough plan to take into account problems on the ground.

In this example, a complicated tile design was chosen for the patio, so the width of the boundary border had to be adjusted so that only half-tiles had to be cut, which would significantly reduce breakages and wastage. This kind of detailed planning can save time, trouble and expense at the construction stage.

Pegging the plan out on the ground also revealed that by keeping to the rectangular pattern, insufficient space would have been left for shrubs at the corners, so these were rounded to provide extra planting space.

Many potential problems can be overcome by critical appraisal and minor adjustments at this stage.

MARKING OUT THE LAYOUT

Curved borders can be marked out with a hose-pipe or thick rope, and the curves adjusted so that they look natural and not too acute. Adjustments are easily made by moving the hose or rope until it looks right (see above).

If you plan a tree or large shrub, especially where you want it to mask a view or to be seen as a focal point from various parts of the garden, insert a pole or tall cane in the planned position. This will help you to visualize its effect, and you should be able to judge whether shadows cast over other areas are likely to be a problem.

Once the design has been marked out on the ground, look at it from as many different angles as possible, and at different times of the day. Provided you choose a sunny day, you will see where shadows fall and where shade could be a problem, but bear in mind that the time of year will affect the angle and length of the shadows. So if you are doing this in the winter, do not be too despondent.

Also, always look at your pegged-out plan from each room that overlooks it. The view from an upstairs room can be particularly useful in helping to visualize the overall plan.

Whenever possible, mark out the layout on the ground – this is the closest you can get to visualizing the finished garden.

Straight lines can be marked out with string stretched between pegs or canes, and an impression of a curve can be achieved by using plenty of pegs or canes close together. Alternatively, use a hose-pipe or rope, as described for marking out curved beds. Loose bricks are useful for indicating the outline of raised beds.

The final design plan

No garden design is perfect and you will probably modify it slightly during construction, but it is worth drawing a final scale plan in detail before you order materials and make a physical start. This will enable you to calculate the number of bricks or paving slabs and the amount of other materials accurately (always allow a little extra for wastage).

This is the stage at which you can draw in your planting plans if you prefer. If time and money is limited, it may be better to concentrate on the main construction at this stage, and do the planting later. Much depends on the time of year. If you finish the construction in spring, for example, and want to restrict expenditure on major items like trees and shrubs until the autumn or following spring, you can always fill the spaces with cheerful annuals for the first summer at minimal cost. On the other hand, the sooner these long-term plants are put in, the more quickly your garden will have that sought-after mature and established look.

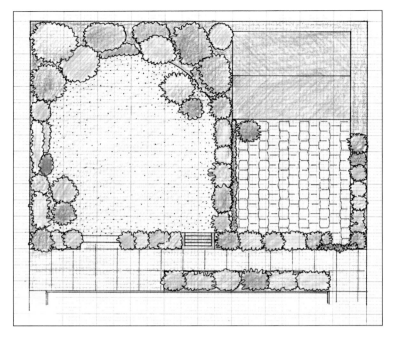

The final plan is the one you will use for construction. Depending on the scale of the plan and size of the garden, you can either mark measurements on the plan or calculate them as necessary from the squared graph paper.
This should be your guide and not your slave, so be prepared to modify dimensions and features as appropriate during construction.

Low raised beds can be used to create the effect of enclosed outdoor "rooms" without keeping out light, but in a small area they need to be softened so that they don't dominate the area. Here herbs in containers have been used to add interest and soften the effect of the new walling. Containers like this need not be considered at the planning stage but can be added afterwards.

It will take several seasons for shrubs, climbers and slow-growing perennials to become established, so fill the gaps with plenty of quick-growing plants for fast results.

Right: If choosing gravel as a surface, select a type that produces the effect you like. Small pea-sized gravel looks very different from the large, angular gravel used in this picture. The actual effect will also depend on whether the gravel is wet or dry, as well as on the light. Some gravels can look very harsh when dry and viewed in bright sunlight.
A large expanse of gravel can look a little bleak, so it's a good idea to plant through it if you think the effect needs softening. This can always be done later, and is probably best improvised rather than planned like a border. Choose plants that grow well in dry conditions.

Preparing a planting plan

The hard landscaping acts like a skeleton and gives a garden its structure, but it is the choice of plants that gives it shape and character. Because plants become too large or straggly, or simply die from disease, the weather, or age, planting is a continuous process. But it is always worth starting with a paper plan rather than be influenced by impulse purchase and then wonder where to put the plants.

1 Start with an outline of the area to be planted, with distances marked on the graph paper to make positioning easier, and some good plant catalogues or books that include plenty of pictures and likely heights and spreads for the plants. Treat likely heights and spreads with caution, as much will depend on where you live and on soil and seasons, but they are a useful guide.

2 If your plant knowledge is good you may be able to draw directly onto your plan, but if you find it easier to move around pieces of paper rather than use a pencil and eraser, cut out shapes to represent the plants that you are planning to include. Write on their height, spread and flowering period if this helps, and mark their name on the back or front.

It will help to colour them – evergreen in green, variegated in say green and gold stripes, golden plants in yellow, and so on. Coloured spots can indicate the colour of any flowers. Visual aids like this will help enormously, but bear in mind that flat shapes on paper give no indication of the shapes of the plants (spiky, rounded, feathery, etc), so you need to bear this in mind when positioning.

Shrubs can be represented as single specimens, but border plants should be planted in groups of threes or fives whenever possible, so that they grow into each other as a drift of colour. Bear this in mind when cutting out your shapes to move around.

3 Position the tall or key plants first. You may have to adjust them when the other plants are added, but it is important to get these plants correctly positioned first as they will probably dominate the finished border.

Add the mid-height plants next, but make sure some of these appear to drift towards the back of the border between the taller ones, to avoid the appearance of a rigid, tiered effect.

Finally, fill in with low-growing plants. The larger the drift of these, the more effective they are likely to be. Individual small plants often lack impact, and can be swamped by more vigorous neighbours.

4 The initial plans can be fairly crude as they merely explore the possibilities of various plant combinations and associations. So, to visualize the final effect more easily, draw your final planting plan in more detail.

1 CREATING THE OUTLINE

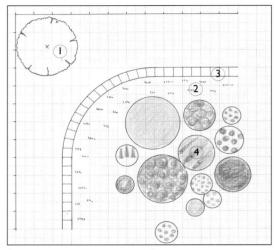

I	Existing flagpole cherry	3	Mowing edge
	(Prunus 'Amanogawa')	4	Cut out plants to fill in
2	Lawn		border

2 ADDING IN THE PLANTS

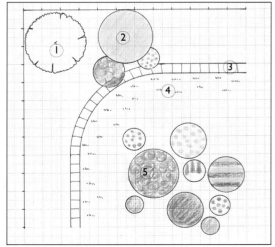

I	Existing flagpole cherry	4	Lawn
	(Prunus 'Amanogawa')	5	Mowing edge
2	Plants in position		
3	Plants still to be positioned		

3 FILLING OUT THE DESIGN

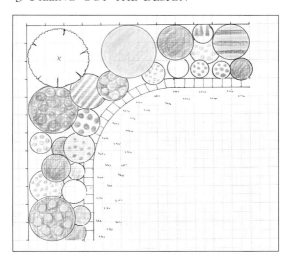

4 COMPLETING THE DETAIL

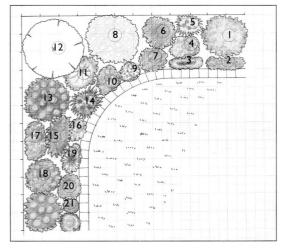

1	*Houttuynia cordata* 'Chameleon' 30cm/1ft	11	*Cornus alba* 'Sibirica' 120cm/4ft
2	Bergenia 30cm/1ft	12	Existing flagpole cherry (*Prunus* 'Amanogawa')
3	*Diascia barberae* 30cm/1ft	13	Camellia 'Donation' (evergreen) 200cm/6ft
4	*Perovskia atriplicifolia* 90cm/3ft	14	Agapanthus 60cm/2ft
5	Kniphofia 120cm/4ft	15	Hosta 45cm/1½ft
6	Rosemary 20cm/1ft	16	Bergenia 30cm/1ft
7	Artemisia 'Powis Castle' 90cm/3ft	17	*Anemone x hybrida* 75cm/2½ft
8	*Choisya ternata* 90cm/3ft	18	Potentilla 'Princess' 75cm/2½ft
9	Dwarf Michaelmas daisy 60cm/2ft	19	Lavender 30cm/1ft
10	Cistus 45cm/1½ft	20	Stachys byzantina 30cm/1ft
		21	Mahonia 'Charity' (evergreen) 240cm/8ft

GREEN-FINGERED RULES OF THUMB

- Be careful to ensure that tall plants are not placed in front of smaller ones. Heights given in books and catalogues can only be a guide, however, so be prepared for surprises.

- Place tall plants at the back of the border whenever possible (or in the centre of an island bed viewed from both sides), but avoid regimented tiers. A few plants that stand above the others in the middle or towards the front of the border often look good.

- Plant herbaceous plants in groups of at least three plants whenever possible. Even in a small area, a group of the same kind of plant will probably have more impact than the same number of plants of different kinds.

- Use plenty of foliage plants – they will remain attractive for much longer than most flowering kinds.

- Do not be afraid to mix shrubs and herbaceous plants – your borders will almost certainly look more interesting throughout the year. Do not overlook the role of bulbs too, especially bold ones like crown imperials (*Fritillaria imperialis*) and lilies.

- Use plenty of carpeters along the edge and to fill in gaps between large plants. It is better to cover the ground with these than to allow weeds to grow.

COLOUR SCHEMES

- Single-colour theme borders (or combinations of sympathetic colours, such as blue and mauve with grey or silver) are popular in large gardens, but difficult to achieve where space is limited and as much variety as possible has to be crammed in.

- If space is limited, it is worth concentrating light-coloured plants with golden leaves or foliage that is variegated with a pale colour in those parts of the garden that are rather shady and dull.

- If colour schemes are important to you, try creating clusters of interesting colour combinations or harmonies in parts of the border. A group of three, four or five plants that look good together can have a similar effect to a colour-theme border.

Outdoor rooms

Your garden will be much more interesting if it cannot all be seen at once. Whether you have an entirely different style in each area (for example, a wild border or a romantic, secluded corner) or variations on the basic theme, the more it has to be explored, like the rooms of a house, the more fascinating it becomes.

This principle also applies to a small garden, when it can be even more valuable as a design technique. A small garden, such as the one shown here, where everything can be taken in at a quick glance is likely to be boring, but if you have to go around a few screens, negotiate a few bends or obstacles, it will hold many more surprises.

Right: *As the photograph shows, this garden is narrow, but sometimes even a narrow garden can be divided in both directions. This avoids the banded effect that would result if all the divisions were horizontal across the garden with no vertical divisions to balance them out.*

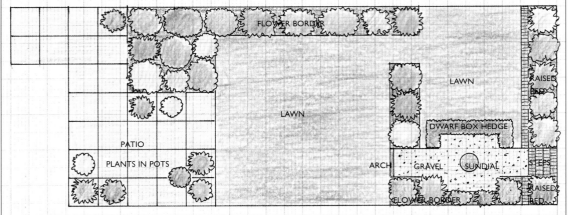

Left: *In plan view the simplicity of this design is obvious, yet the slight changes of level and height provided by shrubs and the low hedge all help to give the impression of moving from room to room, with a series of gardens within the garden.*

Left: *By placing the arch and the steps at the end of the garden off-centre, a vista has been produced that runs along the whole length of the garden, as seen from the patio. This gives the garden a sense of depth and size, even though areas have been partitioned off for individual exploration.*

Above: *Raised beds and a gravelled area add more variety and a sense of enclosure, and provide a good point from which to view the garden, as the picture shows. The small gravelled area would have been impractical as grass, but the gravel is an ideal surface for this situation. Different surface textures are important in creating the sense of walking into different areas.*

Patio pleasures

Patios are popular because they bridge the gap between house and garden, and even though they are sometimes located remotely from the house, they provide an opportunity to "live" in the garden. They are great for entertaining, and are a perfect place to sit, relax and admire the rest of your garden. Patios are for people, but they should be places for plants too. Be prepared to spend time planning a patio that will look beautiful and not boring. The more "room-like" you make it, the more effective it will be as a place to relax or entertain in.

Situating a patio next to the house, with adjoining patio doors or French windows, integrates house and garden and makes it an extension of the living area. Choosing a surface such as timber decking or glazed tiles also helps to tie it more closely as an extension of the house in a way that is difficult to achieve with paving slabs or clay pavers.

If a room opens onto the patio, it is more practical to use stylish and upholstered chairs as they can easily be moved indoors at the end of the day.

Sometimes, however, simplicity is appropriate, especially if the patio is located away from the house. An area paved with bricks or clay pavers often blends more sympathetically with the surrounding garden than concrete blocks or slabs, and if any pillars for a patio overhead are made from bricks, the design will look well-integrated and carefully planned.

In a large garden, setting the patio at a 45-degree angle to the house can be very effective. It helps to join two sides of the garden, while at the same time linking house and garden over a broad angle. In this example, the angle has been emphasized by the use of rows of bricks that take the eye across the patio.

Mixing materials, such as bricks and paving slabs, creates a more interesting surface texture than using just one kind of paving. Do not use more than three different kinds of paving, however, otherwise the effect may look fussy and confused.

The more "room-like" you can make a patio, the cosier and more intimate it will appear as a place to sit and relax or to entertain friends. Useful techniques to use are a wall to give a sense of enclosure and a change of level or a "gateway" to the rest of the garden. Paving that simply butts onto the lawn at the same level tends to look boring, and the patio lacks impact because it has no clear-cut boundary.

When not actually used for entertaining, this kind of paved area is often best furnished with just a few simple, but elegant, chairs. The use of space can bring its own sense of tranquillity.

An abundant use of containers helps to make a patio look furnished and welcoming, but they add considerably to the maintenance required. Patio plants should always look in tip-top condition, which demands regular watering, feeding and dead-heading.

TIPS FOR A TIP-TOP PATIO

- Make sure it is large enough to be able to move around freely, even when you have a few guests. If it is heavily planted and has a lot of furniture, you may need to allow a little extra space.

- Choose a sunny position, away from overhanging trees (midges, leaves and drips after a shower can all be problems).

- Provide shelter from wind. If on an exposed site, or near a wind tunnel – perhaps between houses – provide a windbreak. A screen block wall, with shrubs in front, can be decorative and will filter the wind. Solid brick walls can look oppressive if tall, but a low wall can be effective, as you are often less exposed when sitting.

- Give your patio clear boundaries – a low wall or a raised bed, even an ornamental hedge or dwarf shrubs can be used. If the patio is large, a balustrade can look impressive. A simple change of level, with a step up or down to the rest of the garden, is a good way to create the illusion of a boundary while maintaining a seamless link with the rest of the garden.

- Consider having a patio overhead, especially if the patio adjoins the house. This can provide shade in summer if it is covered with a vine or climber (nothing with spines or long, cascading shoots however).

Ground cover for texture

Ground cover is popular as an attractive means of suppressing weeds, but it can also be used as a design element. Any plant that provides a carpet-like, even covering of the soil can be used for its textural effect.

Ground-cover plants that form a dense, compact carpet of even height can be used to create texture as well as a means of suppressing weeds. They are most useful in a big garden, where large areas can be covered, and ground-cover plants with different colours and textures create a kind of patchwork, but they also have a role in small gardens.

If you want a low-maintenance garden with a strong sense of design, but no regular weeding, planting and watering, they can be used as a living alternative to paving. The garden illustrated below could have been paved and would have looked very dull. By planting *Pachysandra terminalis*, however, it has become eye-catching.

Consider ground-cover plants where you simply want to cover an area of ground without the cost and effort of laying paving, or if you simply find the effect of paving too harsh and boring.

PLANTING THROUGH A SHEET

Planting through a mulching sheet will help to suppress weeds and conserve moisture during the vital first year or two while the plants become well established. You can use black polythene, which is cheap, but a proper mulching sheet like the one shown here is better as it allows water to penetrate.

Some ground-cover plants – those that spread by underground stems or that throw up new plants from their roots – should not be planted through a mulching sheet. You want to encourage these plants to colonize an area by throwing up new plants a short distance from the parent.

1 Always prepare the ground well, incorporating a generous amount of organic material such as rotted manure or garden compost. Rake in a slow-release fertilizer, and make sure the ground is thoroughly watered.
Fix the sheet into position by tucking the edges into the ground and covering with soil. To plant, simply make two slits in the form of a cross, large enough to accommodate the root-ball.

2 Excavate a hole with a trowel – or a spade if the plants are large – then plant normally. Always make sure the plant has been thoroughly watered in its container at least half an hour before planting, and water it again once the soil has been firmed around the roots.

3 A mulching sheet is very practical, but not attractive. If you find it off-putting while the plants are growing together (which will probably take several seasons), cover it with a decorative mulch such as chipped bark. This will not have to be applied as thickly as if used without the sheet, as its function is purely decorative.

Ground-cover plants suppress weeds most effectively (shown here is Pachysandra terminalis*).*

PLANTING GROUND COVER

When they are well established, ground-cover plants will suppress weeds and should not require regular watering. For the first year or two after planting, however, they are as vulnerable as other plants. You must be prepared to water them if the soil is dry, and weeds have to be controlled. When established, they will more than return the favour.

Planting through a mulching sheet, like the one shown opposite, will get them off to a good start by suppressing weeds and conserving moisture, but do not use this method for those plants that spread by sideways growth beneath the ground (such as *pachysandra* and *ajuga*). Instead, mulch these with at least 5cm (2in) of chipped bark or some other attractive mulching material.

Right: *Ground cover at its best contributes a surface texture as well as suppressing weeds. The Pachysandra terminalis used here has all the attributes of a good ground-cover plant: dense, compact, evergreen growth, and a natural spreading habit that knits together to form a carpet, yet is not so rampant that control is difficult. There is also a variegated form of it, but when used like this the plain green can be very attractive.*

Above: *Heathers are one of the best flowering ground covers, and there are many species and varieties that can be used. This one is* Erica carnea. *Ground cover is particularly useful on a sloping site that would be difficult to keep cultivated.*

The grassless garden

For many gardeners, a lawn is the centrepiece of the garden; for others it represents a chore and can become a source of resentment. A grass lawn is still the only practical option for a large area, but in a small garden there are plenty of alternatives to consider. Some of the living alternatives are less practical as areas to walk on, but gravel will stand any amount of wear, and needs practically no maintenance.

This picture shows chamomile, sometimes used in Great Britain and other parts of Europe, but less popular in America as the climate is not so conducive to this use of the plant. It may, however, be successful in moist regions.

Gravel is the most practical option for a small area if you are looking for a minimum-maintenance alternative to grass. Gravels come in many different colours as well as sizes, so choose one that suits the rest of your garden design.

Living substitutes to grass can also be very attractive, but do not expect them to be as hard-wearing and trouble-free as grasses. For a start, you probably will not be able to use selective hormone weedkillers on them, so weeding will be a hand operation, and although they will tolerate some foot traffic, they will not put up with the hard punishment that most grass lawns have to take. For those reasons, these living alternatives to grass are best confined to a small area that is decorative rather than a place for the kids to play football.

Plants to try include chamomile and creeping thymes such as *Thymus serpyllum*, and *Cotula squalida* (this dies back in a cold winter but forms a fresh thick carpet in spring).

The small, rounded gravel used in this garden produces a very smooth finish and is easy to walk on after it is well-compacted. This example shows gravel as a straight alternative to grass, because the area covered used to be a lawn before it was lifted and replaced. The edging that is necessary to retain the gravel and keep it off the flowerbeds emphasizes the gravelled area as a strong design feature in its own right.

Gravel can also be used in a less formal way, so that it flows between the plants and there is no clear-cut edge between a walking area and plant area. This means there are no edges to trim and weeding among the plants is kept to a minimum.

Some people find gravel disconcerting to walk on, but if you find it uncomfortable, try including paving slabs, rather like stepping stones, across the area that you walk on most frequently.

If you use gravel as an alternative to grass, it's a good idea to make a positive feature of it. If the area is large, like this, there is a risk that it can look flat and boring, especially if viewed in harsh sunlight, but strong planting around the edge will help to offset this effect, and the use of a focal point plant within the gravel, like this Cordyline australis, will ensure that your alternative to grass is always an attractive feature.

If you find that trying to control the clover in your grass lawn is a battle that is difficult to win, why not try a small lawn of clover instead of grass? As you will know, it tolerates walking on, and can look quite attractive in summer, and is probably greener than grass in dry weather. White clover (Trifolium repens) is a good one to use for lawns, but you will probably have to buy it from a company specializing in wild flower or agricultural seeds.

Coping with slopes

Sloping sites are particularly difficult to plan on paper, and they are much more challenging to design in general. It is also more difficult to adapt other people's designs as sloping gardens vary so much in the degree of slope – even whether it is up or down – as well as size and aspect. Sloping gardens really do have to be tailor-made to the site as well as to your preferences. You can, however, turn the drawbacks into advantages, as changes of level can add interest and provide an excellent setting for rock gardens and cascading "streams".

PLANNING A DOWNWARD-SLOPING GARDEN

A downward-sloping garden with an attractive view is much easier to design successfully. The view from the house can be the panorama beyond the garden or the garden itself as it falls away below. If the outlook is unattractive, however, it may be advisable to use the lowest part of the garden, well-screened by shrubs and small trees, as the main sitting area.

The plan on the right demonstrates several important principles when designing a sloping garden, and unusually combines terraces with a natural slope. Terracing is expensive and time-consuming: considerable earth-moving is involved and retaining walls on strong foundations have to be constructed. Likewise, simply moving the topsoil from one area to deposit lower down the slope is unsatisfactory as part of the garden will then be left with subsoil at the surface for planting – a recipe for disappointment. Topsoil should be set aside, the underlying ground levelled, and then the topsoil can be returned.

Terracing provides flat areas on which to walk and relax, and this design includes suitable flat areas along the length of the garden, and as these have been used for hard surfaces, the problem of topsoil movement does not arise. By retaining the natural slope for a large part of the garden, cost and structural work has been reduced.

Although there are some retaining walls, the two walls that zigzag down the garden are stepped so that they remain just above the surrounding ground.

Retaining a large area of naturally sloping ground also provides an ideal setting for rock outcrops and an artificial stream with a series of cascades.

Taking a path across the garden at an angle makes it seem less steep. A path that runs in a straight line down the slope only serves to emphasize the drop.

A DOWNWARD-SLOPING GARDEN

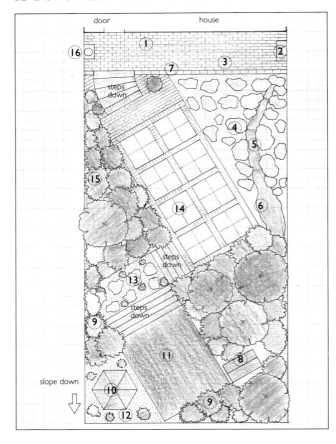

1	Bricks or clay pavers	9	Shrubs
2	Wall fountain with small pool	10	Summerhouse with views across garden
3	Patio		and to attractive view below garden
4	Rock garden bank sloping down-hill and	11	Lawn
	towards flat paved area	12	Gravel with alpines
5	"Stream" with cascades	13	Gravel area with natural paving
6	Pond, disappearing behind shrubs	14	Bricks or clay pavers mixed with
7	Small retaining wall		paving slabs
8	Shed for tools and mower	15	Trees and shrubs
		16	Ornament (on plinth)

AN UPWARD-SLOPING GARDEN

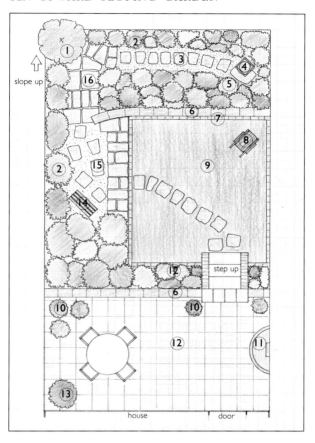

slope up

step up

house   door

I	Small tree	9	Thyme or chamomile lawn
2	Shrubs	10	Plants in containers
3	Natural stone paving slabs set in gravel	11	Wall fountain with small pool beneath
4	Ornament on plinth as focal point	12	Patio
5	Dwarf shrubs on bank	13	Shrub or small tree in large tub
6	Retaining wall	14	Seat
7	Brick edge	15	Natural stone paving slabs set in gravel
8	Lounger or deckchair	16	Natural stone path

PLANNING AN UPWARD-SLOPING GARDEN

An upward slope is more challenging. Distant views are not a possibility and even upper floors may look out onto the bank. Terracing can look oppressive, but a "secret" garden full of meandering paths flanked by shrubs is an effective way to deal with the slope. Some retaining walls are usually necessary, but if planted with shrubs, the effect will be masked and the plants on the lower terraces will hide the upper walls and banks.

With this kind of garden it is important to use focal points to give the paths a purpose; just as a maze has a focal point (its centre).

Lawns are difficult to accommodate on a steeply sloping site, and difficult to mow too, as mowers are awkward to carry up steps and steep ramps for access. It is generally best to avoid them, but in the example shown left a grass alternative has been used to provide a "lawn" in a small levelled area. The chamomile or thyme only requires an occasional trim with shears, which is not an onerous job for a small area.

Steep slopes are ideal for a rock garden. Construction can be difficult, however, and manhandling and positioning rocks safely on a steep slope requires considerable expertise.

A few rocks will go further if presented as outcrops on a grassy bank, and the effect is more natural and less costly. The drawback is the grass that has to be mown between the rock outcrops; it needs a suitable mower and considerable care taken when cutting.

Long and narrow

Long, narrow gardens offer great scope for imaginative design. There are opportunities to divide the garden up into a series of smaller gardens or areas with different themes or styles. Instead of a long, narrow lawn with ribbon beds on either side, break it up into a series of areas to be explored and discovered.

Long, narrow gardens, typical of many older town houses, are often laid out with a design that emphasizes their narrowness. Beds that run the length of the garden and long, narrow lawns make the garden predictable and usually boring. Breaking it up into a series of smaller areas ensures the garden cannot be taken in at a single glance, and it makes it seem cosy and intimate rather than narrow.

The very simple design featured below divides the garden into a series of "rooms", with a trellis and screen-block wall preventing the eye seeing what lies within each section without the oppressiveness of a solid screen.

By including many fragrant shrubs, border plants and annuals in the mixed borders, especially near the garden seats, a fragrant garden can be created, with the scents tending to linger in the enclosed area. The basic design is formal in style, with a long vista leading the eye along to the end of the garden, giving it an impression of size. A simple variation, if you prefer more plants, would be to replace the lawn with border perennials, perhaps mixed with evergreen shrubs.

However you deal with a long, narrow plot, try to break up the garden so that the eye does not go straight down to the end. Make sure there are beds or features that interrupt the straight lines. In this design, two rectangular areas – one paved, the other gravel – have been used to hold interest.

1	Ornament (on plinth)
2	Herb garden
3	Shed
4	Trellis
5	Climbers (e.g. ivy, *parthenocissus* and clematis against trellis)
6	Sundial or birdbath
7	Mixed border
8	Large pot with shrub/shaped clipped box
9	Garden bench
10	Pool with fountain
11	Arch
12	Group of large shrubs (in tubs/large pots)
13	Screen-block wall
14	Patio furniture
15	Vegetable garden
16	Trellis arch
17	Path

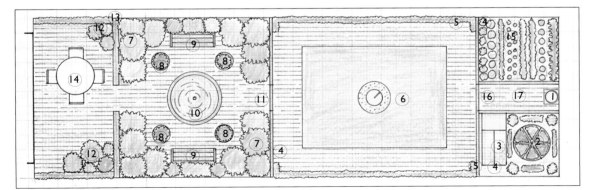

Above: *A focal point towards the centre of the garden also helps to distract the eye from the limiting shape of the garden. The role of this attractive planted urn as a focal point is plain to see.*

Left: *Not everyone likes a formal style with lots of straight edges, but you can achieve a similar effect with flowing informal borders and apparently rambling paths.*

In this garden, the borders along the long sides have been extended into broad, curved sweeps, and island beds with conifers have been used to provide visual "blocks".

This kind of design can be achieved quite easily by modifying an existing long, narrow lawn. The beds can be widened with broad sweeps and island beds cut into the grass. Simple paving and planting does the rest. You don't have to spend a lot of money on hard landscaping to create a more interesting garden.

Dealing with difficult shapes

Owners of rectangular gardens often wish for a more interesting shape with which to work, but gardens with an irregular shape can be particularly difficult to design. Corner sites are common but surprisingly difficult to use imaginatively, while L-shaped gardens are a special challenge if the two "legs" are to be well-integrated. There are as many solutions as there are gardens with these problems, and the two examples here explore just a few design ideas that you could consider.

The pergola effectively "turns" the garden in this design, and manages to look right even though it links two different design styles: the formal rectangular style of house, patio, rectangular lawn and straight-edged flower borders; and the flowing curves of that part of the garden not visible from the house.

Instead of this contrast of styles, you could bring the flower borders that link house with pergola out into the lawn in some gentle curves, or the straight lines of the first section could be carried on into the second. Which option you find most appropriate will be a matter of personal preference.

Instead of a pergola, you could use a summerhouse in the corner, perhaps an octagonal one so that it does not appear to have just one "front", set in the corner. This would make a strong focal point, and from it you could enjoy the view along both sections of your garden.

AN L-SHAPED GARDEN

If your garden is large, you may prefer to treat the two "legs" separately, perhaps keeping the one visible from the house as an ornamental area, and using the other section as a screened-off kitchen garden, or maybe a more informal wild area planted to attract wildlife. This approach can give you the best of both worlds.

If your garden is relatively small, you will probably want to combine the two areas visually to make the most of available space and to make your garden seem as large as possible. The design shown here uses techniques to make the garden seem as large as possible.

It is important to have a strong design element at the point where the two parts of the garden come together. There must be a reason for walking to the end of the garden so that the remaining part unfolds and entices you to explore.

A seat or an interesting water feature are ideal focal points, but in this example a pergola as well as a seat has been used, as a pivot around which the two parts of the garden have been centred.

The pergola makes an attractive focal point viewed from any position in the garden, and its rectangular shape helps to "turn" the axis of the garden in a natural and unobtrusive way.

It is desirable to have another focal point at the far end of the garden to make the most of the whole garden.

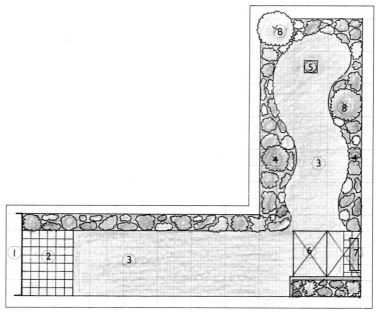

1	House	5	Sundial set on gravel planted with alpines
2	Patio	6	Decorative pergola
3	Lawn	7	Garden seat
4	Flower borders	8	Tree

A CORNER SITE

Corner sites offer lots of scope, but they can be rather "public" unless screened in some way with a fence or hedge. Always check whether this is permissible, however, as there may be restrictions in the deeds of the property or laid down by the highways department concerning the height of hedges, etc. if they are likely to obstruct the view for traffic. Usually, however, you can create a sense of privacy and still keep within any restrictions there may be.

If you want something more intensively designed than say a lawn that sweeps around the house, it is worth trying to create a design that integrates the two sides. In this example, a design based on a grid diagonal to the house has been used to take full advantage of the long dimension across the garden, while at the same time using shrubs to mask the curved boundary, which also gives privacy.

If this highly structured design does not appeal to you, a more informal style with lawn and sweeping beds could be used.

I	Back garden	9	Dwarf hedge
2	House	10	Shrubs and border plants
3	Screen-block wall	II	Plants
4	Gate	12	Front door
5	Shrubs	13	Drive
6	Hedge	14	Coloured slabs and plants in containers
7	Ornament	15	Lawn
8	Garden seat	16	Pond

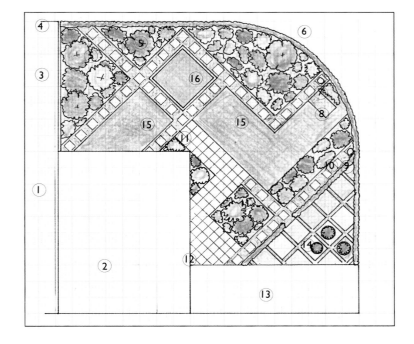

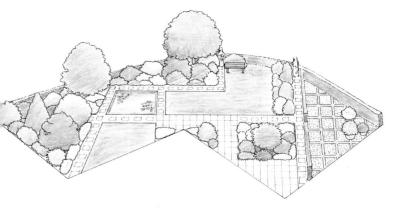

In this design it is the paths that lay the foundation for the diagonal pattern, so they have been given strong visual impact. As continuous paving slabs would look boring as well as uninspiring, they have been spaced and set into a wider area of gravel. By using fine or coarse gravel, or even small beach pebbles, the character of the paths can be changed to suit individual preference.

The extra depth given to the planting areas by their angular shape provides scope for planting small trees or large specimen shrubs to add height and a greater sense of structure.

A sense of fun

Gardens tend to reflect the personality of their owners, and if you have a fun personality or a sense of humour, you will probably want to express that in the way your garden is planned.

Eccentric gardens are not to everyone's taste, but subtle humour can be achieved in odd corners or through tasteful focal points that hint at that sense of mischief.

If the structure of a garden has a bold, even eccentric, appearance, it will make a bold statement regardless of the plants. It needs confidence, however, because done half-heartedly it may seem cranky rather than clever.

The garden on the opposite page could look rather green and dull with an ordinary arch, path, traditional raised bed and container, especially in winter. The choice of colours and materials, however, ensures that this garden looks spectacular, whatever the season.

The garden does not readily conform to the design principles commonly suggested, but its charm lies in its defiance of tradition, and any suggestion of straight lines or even symmetry of curves would be out of place. Even the path has been laid in a way that challenges orthodoxy. It is a straight path with bricks that follow a curving, snake-like pattern. The arch, too, demands attention. A normal arch would be attractive with a clematis in flower, but this one cries out to be noticed at all times.

Ornaments can be used among the plants in borders too, where their very unexpectedness adds an extra dimension. Moving them around periodically also adds to their unpredictability. Use them to add drama to an area of the garden that lacks impact: the berberis in this picture are unexciting, but the boy crawling out from between the bushes immediately makes this a magical part of the garden.

Small ornaments offer enormous scope because they are easily moved around until they look right. You can even reposition them on a regular basis to add variety to your garden.

These two birds change a fairly ordinary garden scene into something special. They act as a focal point, but their positioning as a pair also gives them a light-hearted look.

These flowers would look attractive in a group of ordinary pots, but their fun containers will almost certainly bring a smile to the face. Gardening has its lighter moments, so do not waste the opportunity to bring a breath of fresh air to potentially gloomy corners.

Above: *Even in a conventional or traditional garden there is scope for the unexpected, especially if it brings a smile or creates a focal point in an otherwise dull spot. These "sunflowers" are in a shady position at the end of a path that leads to an uninteresting fence. If you imagine the picture without the focal point, this is immediately seen as a dull part of the garden.*

Flowers like this can be cut from marine ply, or other weatherproof material, and painted before being fixed in position.

A feature like this will almost certainly generate comment, some favourable some unfavourable, it depends on an individual's sense of humour. If you have a sense of fun, however, you won't be deterred from trying something a little different.

Left: *Not everyone could live with this kind of garden, but if it works for you it's right. Challenging the senses is a good idea, but you need confidence to do it on this scale.*

With children in mind

Gardens are seldom designed for children, but they should sometimes be designed with children in mind. Small children pose special problems of safety if you are planning water features, young children require safe play areas, and older children can be tough on a garden if they do not have an area where the grass and the plants are not easily damaged.

If you are planning to stay in your home for many years, however, it pays to plan with the long term in mind too. Features that are suitable for the children can often be converted into a more ornamental part of the garden when the offspring have grown up.

A "Wendy house" is always popular with children, but positioned in a conspicuous part of the garden, it can dominate the scene and detract from the design and the plants. If you paint it attractively, in a light colour, it can be used as a focal point in a less obvious corner of the garden.

Bear in mind, however, that you may prefer to have it within easy sight and earshot of the house.

Trampolines and large activity toys like swings are always difficult to accommodate, and they will mar the most well-designed garden if placed in a prominent position.

If you have a large lawn with borders along the side, try bringing the border out in a couple of grand sweeps, so that a large bay of lawn is hidden once shrubs and screening plants have grown up.

Children like a sense of adventure, and older children will appreciate a tree house as much as younger ones love a "Wendy house". An old tree that forks close to ground level is ideal, as the house will then be easier to construct and safer to play in. A tree house is something that a responsible adult should construct, not a child.

TOUGH LAWNS, TOUGH PLANTS

- Play lawns require tough grasses – avoid seed mixtures or turf of the type used for bowling greens and immaculately kept lawns. You can still enjoy a quality lawn that will look green and lush (provided you water it in dry weather), and the modern strains of hard-wearing grasses are much finer and more attractive than the older ones, which were often rather coarse.

- Shrubs are a better choice than bedding plants until the children are old enough to respect the boundaries of play, but avoid those with thorns and beware of any that can cause severe allergies if they come into contact with exposed skin – such as rue (*Ruta graveolens*).

Small children love a sandpit, and if the children are of that age, a pond is not a good idea (you can make them secure with metal protection, but this kills the natural beauty of the pond). If you intend to build a pond when the children are a little older, it makes sense to construct a sandpit that can be converted into a pond later. The sandpit illustrated could easily be visualized as a pond when its present function is redundant.

Always make sure there is free drainage at the bottom while being used as a sandpit, otherwise it will become waterlogged after heavy rain. And make a lid to fit over it when not in use, otherwise animals such as cats will foul it.

In cottage-garden style

Cottage gardens are difficult to define, yet a garden with the attributes of a cottage garden is instantly recognisable. The emphasis is on dense planting, with a bias towards perennial border plants, and the "design" lies more in the planting than the structure of the garden. They usually look uninspiring in plan view – frequently two wide borders with a path down the middle between gate and door. If your interest lies more in the plants than the hard landscaping, a cottage-garden style could be the solution.

In the garden shown here, the plants are all border perennials – in effect large herbaceous borders – but traditionally there would be lots of annuals such as calendulas and love-in-a-mist (nigella) too.

A typical cottage garden is extremely simple in design – often straight, but wide borders and little else. If your garden is squat, square, and small, you can create a similar effect by treating the whole area like a large border, with a path running around the edge.

To create the appropriate period atmosphere, keep to species or early hybrids rather than highly-bred plants that look too modern. Delphiniums, oriental poppies and achilleas, along with plants such as border pinks and lady's mantle (*Alchemilla*) were commonplace in country gardens and will help to create the style and "atmosphere" that you are seeking.

An old building and roses around the door clearly help, but you can create cottage garden borders in a modern setting if you use another part of the garden, rather than the house, as a backdrop.

PLANTING SUGGESTIONS

Use the two schemes opposite as a guide for your own cottage garden border. Do not follow them slavishly, but add plants that you prefer (provided they are appropriate), and drop those that you do not like. Each of these borders is approximately 3.6m x 1.8m (12ft x 6ft), so you may have to drop some plants if your border is smaller. The borders are shown as mature, with clumps of border perennials that have been established for some years – you may be able to accommodate the same number of plants in a smaller space if you lift and divide more frequently.

In many cases, more than one plant is represented by the areas shown in the borders opposite (border plants are generally best planted in groups of three to five of each kind if there is space). The lupins, for example, represent the bold drift of a number of plants.

These are just some of the cottage garden plants that you could use: there are many more. Remember to keep to types that would have been around, say, 50 years ago or more: do not use modern hybrid lilies in place of the *Lilium regale* shown here, for example.

Hardy perennials shown in the borders include aquilegia, bear's breeches (*Acanthus mollis*), bergamot (*Monarda didyma*), bleeding heart (*Dicentra spectabilis*), catmint (*Nepeta*), coral bells (*Heuchera sanguinea*), delphinium, flag iris, gaillardia, geum, globe thistle (*Echinops ritro*), hollyhock, lady's mantle (*Alchemilla*), lupin, Michaelmas daisy, oriental poppy (*Papaver orientale*), herbaceous peony, perennial gypsophila, pinks, pyrethrum, red hot poker (*kniphofia*), regal lily (*Lilium regale*), sea holly (*Eryingium bourgatii*), shasta daisy (*Chrysanthemum maximum*), sneezewort (*Achillea ptarmica*), viola and yarrow (*Achillea filipendulina*).

Biennials used are Canterbury-bells and foxgloves. Annuals are cornflowers, pot marigolds (*Calendula*), sunflowers (*Helianthus*), and Virginia stocks (*Malcolmia maritima*).

COTTAGE BORDER PLAN A

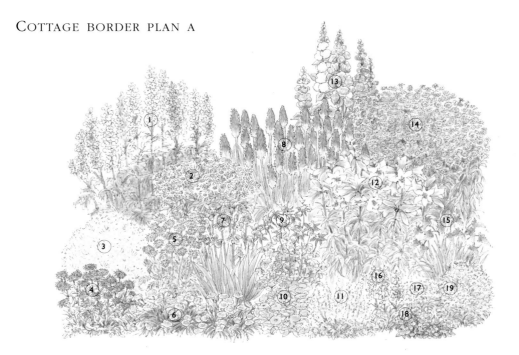

1	Delphinium
2	Shasta daisy (*Chrysanthemum maximum*)
3	Gypsophila
4	Gaillardia
5	Pyrethrum
6	Pinks or border carnations (*Dianthus*)
7	Flag iris
8	Red hot poker (*Kniphofia*)
9	Aquilegia
10	Pot marigolds (*Calendula*)
11	Coral bells
12	Regal lily
13	Hollyhock
14	Michaelmas daisy (*Aster*)
15	Crocosmia
16	Canterbury-bells (*Campanula*)
17	Virginia stocks (*Malcomia*)
18	Viola cornuta
19	Sneezewort (*Achillea ptarmica*)

COTTAGE BORDER PLAN B

1a	Delphinium
2a	Foxglove (*Digitalis*)
3a	Yarrow (*Achillea filipendulina*)
4a	Geum
5a	Catmint (*Nepeta*)
6a	Lupin
7a	Globe thistle (*Echinops*)
8a	Oriental poppy (*Papaver*)
9a	Peony
10a	Sea holly (*Eryngium*)
11a	Cornflower (*Centaurea*)
12a	Lavender (*Lavendula*)
13a	Bleeding heart (*Dicentra spectabilis*)
14a	Lady's mantle (*Alchemilla*)
15a	Bergamot (*Monarda didyma*)
16a	Flag iris
17a	Bear's breeches (*Acanthus*)
18a	Sunflowers (*Helianthus*)

Creating a secluded courtyard

Privacy and seclusion is something most of us appreciate at some time, and it can be even more precious when we are relaxing in the garden. Even in a country garden without over-looking neighbours, it is nice to have a cosy and secluded corner that feels snug and enclosed, but in a town or city it may be the whole garden that needs to be encapsulated in its own private "cocoon", a private green oasis among the surrounding buildings.

There are two fundamental approaches to a courtyard or tiny town garden: the formal one that depends on structures such as walls for privacy, like the one shown on the opposite page (*top*), or an informal approach that depends on the lush growth of trees and shrubs. The picture on page 47 (*bottom*), is a good example of a garden designed with this approach: the sitting area in the centre is like a clearing in woodland.

This type of dense planting with tall-growing shrubs and small trees can become very shady in summer, but on a hot day this can be a welcome attribute. It is also a super way to enjoy a lot of plants in a small area – provided you are willing to cut back and prune fairly ruthlessly on a regular basis, you can pack in a surprising number of plants in a small area, but concentrate on shade-lovers.

Often, however, it's impossible to pretend that your garden is anywhere other than in a town or city, surrounded by other buildings, in which case a formal style that makes a bold and challenging statement despite its surroundings is a pleasing solution.

Tall walls are an asset. They have a sense of age and permanence that a fence never gives, and they can be taller. If well constructed and wide, you can even stand pots and finials on top, especially where there are supporting columns. Walls also provide an ideal support for climbers and for trained fruit or ornamental wall shrubs.

Whether you want to draw attention to the tops of the walls with ornaments or plants will depend on the background. If it is particularly unattractive, it is advisable to draw the eye down into the garden and not upwards to its perimeter.

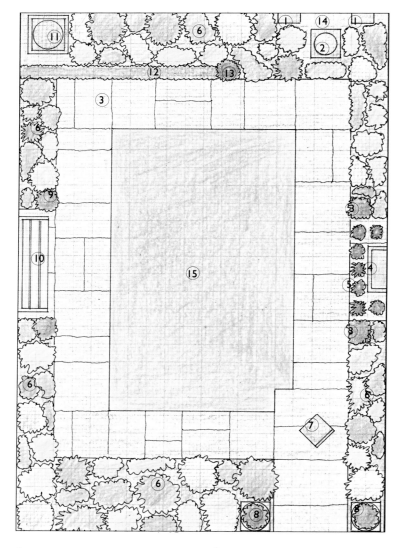

1	Pillars covered with ivy and topped with finials	8	Clipped box in pots on plinths
2	Urn on pedestal	9	Box spiral
3	Natural paving stones	10	White garden seat
4	Wall fountain	11	Large urn on pedestal
5	Box balls in pots	12	Dwarf box hedge
6	Border plants	13	Clipped and shaped box
7	Garden chair	14	Decorative trellis covering old gate
		15	Lawn

Left: *If you decide on a classical or period style like this, it is advisable to use materials that do it justice. There is not a lot of hard landscaping, so be prepared to pay for natural stone paving, and invest in a few ornaments that do the garden justice. Trained and clipped box like these specimens can be expensive, but you will not have to spend much on shrubs for the rest of the garden. And because there are few areas for which you will have to buy seasonal plants, the ongoing costs will be minimal.*

Right: *The designer here has chosen a strong rectangular theme for the paved area, to contrast with the luxuriant and overhanging plants that soften the straight lines. The choice of plain square slabs, arranged in unstaggered rows, gives the design a simple, uncluttered appearance.*

Opposite page: *The essentials of this design are simplicity and restraint, with the emphasis on shape and form provided by the urns and shaped box plants. Add touches of seasonal colour in small containers that can be moved around the garden to suit the season and the mood.*

In Japanese style

True Japanese gardens, designed according to the strict rules of this specialized type of gardening, should only be tackled after much research and study of the subject, as the placing of stones and positioning of particular lanterns have special meanings. And if you want to avoid high maintenance, give raked sand a miss too. It is perfectly possible to create a garden that simply has a strong Japanese influence, however, and it does not matter if you break a few "rules", provided it looks good and has that distinctive Japanese character.

The seasonal variations in a Japanese garden are subtle rather than dramatic. Water, rocks and ornaments can vary in appearance according to the light, but the emphasis is on shape, form and texture, rather than bright colours from flowers.

In a large garden the Japanese influence can be achieved by the use of bridges, lanterns and features like deer-scarers within a landscaped area that includes plenty of plants such as Japanese acers, bamboos, and suitably placed rocks. It is much more difficult to create that kind of garden in a small space, but a formal shape like the one shown here (*opposite above right*) can be very successful in creating an oriental style modified to suit a small Western backyard.

It is important to choose plants that fit the image, like small acers, small pines, azaleas, camellias, small ornamental grasses and dwarf bamboos, and Japanese irises (*I. ensata*). Moss adds to the effect, but thrives best in moist conditions out of direct sun. If mosses cannot be encouraged to grow, try moss-like plants such as *Sagina subulata* (syn. *S. glabra*) and *S. procumbens*. The ground-hugging carpeter *Soleirolia soleirolii* (syn. *Helxine soleirolii*) will also produce a similar affect, but has the drawback of being rampant where winters are mild and conditions suit, and prone to winter losses in very cold areas.

The addition of bonsai trees in pots helps to reinforce the strong Japanese theme.

Always try to choose individual rocks for a Japanese garden, as they form an integral part of the "Japaneseness". If you just leave it to a supplier to select and deliver, they may lack the necessary shape and form to make useful focal points.

A JAPANESE-STYLE GARDEN PLAN

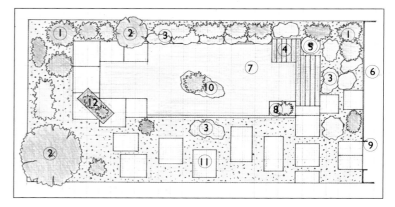

1	Dwarf shrubs and plants	7	Water
2	Japanese acer	8	Bonsai in pot
3	Rocks	9	Door
4	Timber flat bridge	10	Rock with bonsai
5	Lantern	11	Large paving slabs set in gravel
6	House	12	Low display table, in style of timber bridge with bonsai in pot

IN SEARCH OF AUTHENTICITY

- If you want to make your oriental garden as authentic as possible, buy or borrow several books on Japanese gardening. Do not be put off by the Japanese words that you will find sprinkled throughout the text, all you want from them is the meaning and the philosophy that lies behind this form of gardening. It may become a fascinating hobby, and you will start to position the rocks with more care as you realize the symbolic significance of the various aspects of this kind of garden.

- Your garden is unlikely to be judged by an expert, or even a native Japanese, so it does not really matter if the symbolic significance passes you by. The only real test is whether it pleases you.

- Send for the catalogues and brochures produced by specialists in Japanese features such as lanterns, deer-scarers, and bamboo and rock ornaments. These will provide you with plenty of inspiration.

Above: *Use plants with restraint, but make the most of their shape and outline. The juxtaposition of the reed-like leaves of the water plant, rounded lantern, and angular rock is what gives this grouping so much impact. Surface textures are also important, with the strong lines of the red timber bridge contrasting with the fine gravel.*

Below: *This stand for displaying bonsai trees reflects the material and style of the bridge at the other end of the pond. Keep the style simple and uncluttered, and do not over-plant if you want to retain the typical Japanese style of gardening.*

Above: *Fine gravel is an ideal ground covering, much more Japanese in style than the same garden set in a grass lawn. It also helps to make this kind of garden a good choice for low maintenance.*

Ways with water

Water has a fascination for most of us, and there is almost always a way to introduce it into your design. If you have small children, it might be best to confine water to wall-spouts and self-contained wall fountains, or to bubble fountains where the water runs into a hidden reservoir. If you do not have young children to consider, however, there are plenty of imaginative ways to use water.

A conventional garden pond is the first choice for anyone who wants to grow aquatic plants and encourage wildlife. A pond is more than just a water feature; it is a living community of plants, fish, insects and amphibians. By placing it in the foreground of the garden, it is also a dominant element in its design.

The sound of running water is an added attraction, but in a small pond a fountain or cascade can cause water turbulence that is to the detriment of plants such as waterlilies, and probably some of the insect and amphibian visitors too. A simple trickle of water will be enough to create the magical sound of running water, yet by the time it has trickled around the sphere, disturbance within the pond will be minimal.

Water can be used as an "architectural" feature. Plants will not thrive in a small pond like this with constant turbulence from the fountain, and the scope for introducing fish is limited. None of this matters, however, when it is being used primarily as a focal point as part of the hard landscaping.

It is the sight and sound of the water that gives this corner so much impact, and the background planting acts as a frame that softens the background and helps to make a potentially uninspiring corner by the house one of the focal points of the garden.

When positioning moving water like this close to the house, make sure the sound does not become an irritation. Some sounds that are pleasant for a short time can be annoying over a long period.

Water used in a very formal setting, with the simple sound of a gentle trickle rather than the rush of a geyser, adds a sense of tranquillity.

In this situation, the water is a texture, and is best left unplanted. The open surface plays a similar role to the surrounding Pachysandra terminalis *ground cover, and the neatly clipped hedges. In this kind of garden, light and shade, symmetry and texture are all part of its beauty, and it is appropriate either for a corner of a large garden or as the centrepiece of a small town or city garden.*

Still water also has its charm, especially in a formal setting or where there is a definite "architectural" design, where shape, form and texture are strong elements.

This small area shows many good design principles: the excitement of a change of level, contrasting textures for the garden floor (brick and timber, with black mortar to enhance the bricks), water used as a texture and to act like a mirror, and the use of lush green plants and white-painted walls to compensate for the lack of colourful flowers.

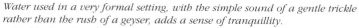

Going wild

Most of us like to encourage wildlife into the garden. You can encourage wildlife simply by feeding the birds, making a pond, and growing plants that butterflies are attracted to. A true wildlife enthusiast will want to go one step further, however, and design the garden with wildlife in mind. Whether this kind of gardening appeals depends on whether you can look at buttercups and daisies and see them as attractive wild flowers, or only as weeds.

A more acceptable compromise for many are normal flower borders given over mainly to wild flowers. Here various poppies and forget-me-nots have self-seeded to provide an undisturbed wild area that is visually attractive and easily managed. Some weeding may be necessary to prevent particularly rampant weeds taking over the bed or border, but generally a bed like this will look after itself.

It is worth clearing the area of weeds first, leaving it for weed seedlings to germinate before weeding again, then sowing a wild flower seed mixture. In this way you are more likely to have a bed with a good range of attractive wild flowers rather than the dominant local weeds.

A wildlife pond usually looks rather overgrown, but that's how it should be. Wildlife is less attracted to large areas of clear water with fountains and cascades than to areas of still water almost congested with plant growth.

It is also important to have some shelter close to the pond, such as a border, an area with bog plants, or even a hedge. Wildlife is much more vulnerable in an open position, but choose a bright position rather than one in dense shade.

Although shape is relatively unimportant, some shallow beach edges are crucial, so that amphibians and other creatures can gain access to the water easily, and climb out without difficulty. An area of shallow water will also encourage birds and other animals to use the pond for drinking.

Whether you could live with this as part of your back lawn depends on the relative appeal of gardening against wildlife. If you like a neat and tidy garden with lots of flowerbeds, this kind of wildlife feature will not appeal. But even a small area of long grass like this will encourage a wide range of birds (especially when seeds ripen), insects and mammals. You should also be able to introduce many attractive wild flowers into an area like this, and of course there is less lawn to mow!

Many common garden plants will attract butterflies, especially Buddleia davidii, *the butterfly-bush. Other common flowers attract butterflies too: this is a small tortoiseshell on a hyacinth.*

Left: *If you have a large garden with space for an orchard or woodland area, creating this kind of wild garden is easy. You need only cut the long grass areas once or twice a year, and let nature do the rest. If there are rare flowers among the buttercups and daisies, you will have to time any cutting carefully to avoid interfering with their natural growth cycles; some parts can be left completely uncultivated. This will attract a wide range of wildlife, most of which will venture into the more ornamental part of the garden as well.*

Finding a home for herbs

No garden is complete without its complement of herbs, and finding a suitable place for them should be considered at the planning stage. A special herb garden is ideal, and can be a highly decorative feature, but many herbs make good container plants, and many are pretty enough to be grown in borders along with the ornamentals. You can simply grow herbs in the kitchen garden together with the vegetables, but why not make more of a feature of them?

A formal herb garden divided into "compartments" like the one featured on the right is practical and a powerful focal point. Separating the various herbs makes cultivation much easier, as some are annuals, some perennials, some self-seed prolifically and if surrounded by soil, these seedlings can become weeds, and others have spreading roots or stems that benefit from containment.

The suggested planting in this plan should be treated only as a starting point for your own choice. There is little point in growing herbs that you do not use unless they are particularly decorative. If you use a lot of one kind of herb, allocate more than one area. There is space for 24 different herbs in this design, but you may prefer to grow only the dozen that you use most often and create a mirror image in the two halves of the herb garden.

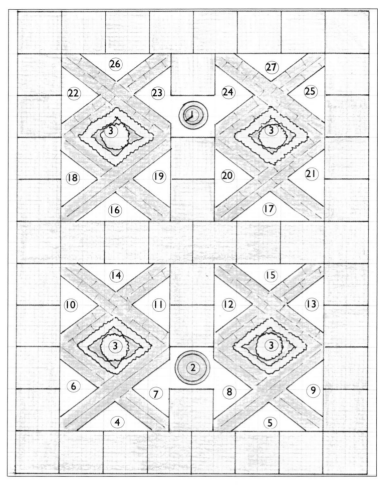

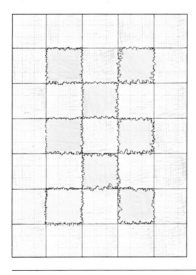

Left: *A chequerboard herb garden can be very effective for a paved area. It has a strong visual impact, and you can easily keep each herb contained within its own small plot while still being able to walk among them.*

1	Sundial	14	Winter savory
2	Birdbath	15	Lavender
3	Dwarf box hedge with bay in centre	16	Thyme
	Suggested planting	17	Borage
4	Summer savory	18	Chives
5	Variegated lemon balm	19	Golden marjoram
6	Variegated apple mint	20	Rosemary
7	Purple sage	21	Mint
8	Cotton lavender	22	Caraway
9	Parsley	23	Bergamot
10	Hyssop	24	Sweet basil
11	French tarragon	25	Chervil
12	Sorrel	26	Garlic
13	Oregano	27	Pot marigold (*Calendula*)

Left: *The herb garden can become a decorative part of the overall garden design. Bear in mind that herb gardens can be a trifle dull in winter, however, as most of the plants will have died down, so they are best used to create interest in a part of the garden that you suddenly discover. Most herbs prefer to be in full sun, so try to choose a position that is in good light for most of the day.*

Below: *There's always space for a few herbs, even if you have to put them in containers. This group of pots contains chives, French tarragon and winter savory.*

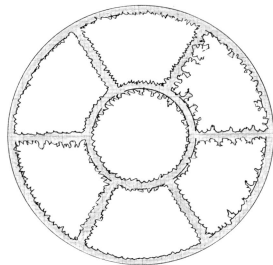

Above: *Where space is limited, a herb wheel is a popular choice. Proper cart wheels can be used, but as these are hard to obtain a similar effect can be achieved with the use of bricks. Plant a different herb in each space created by the spokes.*

The kitchen garden

The traditional kitchen garden demands little design but lots of planning for crop positioning and rotation. Usually an area out of sight of the main ornamental part of the garden is set aside and the crops are grown in straight rows. This simplifies crop rotation and makes cultivation easier – you can weed more easily between straight rows, and it is easier to give each specific crop the appropriate fertilizer and supplementary water when it is required. If you want to make vegetable growing a more high-profile part of your garden, however, you may have to be bold.

Dedicated areas set aside for traditional rows of vegetables make cultivation relatively simple, but integrating flowers and vegetables can be an interesting experiment. It also may help reduce the level of pest and disease infestation that often comes with large areas devoted to a small range of plants.

A potager is a striking way to combine vegetables and flowers, and though expensive to construct and time-intensive to maintain (lots of dwarf box hedging to plant and clip, for instance), it can be justified if it forms a main feature. In a large garden you can enclose the area with hedges, but in a small garden you may want to make this the whole of your design. This is most likely to appeal if your interest lies as much in cooking and a love of fresh vegetables as in ornamental gardening.

The term *jardin potager* is French for "kitchen garden", but the word "potager" has come to mean primarily a kitchen garden that usually contains both vegetables and fruit, laid out ornamentally and often with the beds edged with low hedges like a parterre.

On the other hand, the traditional vegetable plot can be improved simply by giving it a structure with paths. The design on the right is ideal if you want to practise the 1.2m (4ft) bed "no-dig" system, where cultivation is done by reaching across from the paths so that the soil is not compacted.

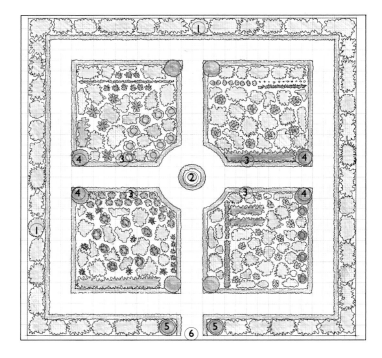

1	Flower border around edge
2	Ornament
3	Dwarf box hedge
4	Topiary shapes
5	Large clipped box
6	Gate/entrance

This design is a more decorative vegetable plot. The use of an ornament such as a birdbath or sundial in the centre emphasizes the formality of this type of vegetable garden.

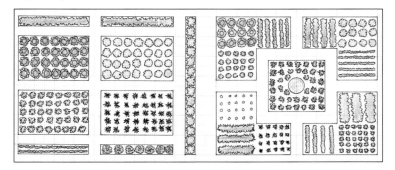

In a potager like this, you can devote the main beds purely to vegetables, and even grow them in straight rows in the conventional manner, but if you want to be bold, try growing flowers and vegetables together.

Many vegetables are ornamental enough to be used in flower borders, among bedding plants, and even in containers – like this rhubarb chard planted alongside lobelia.

This method of growing vegetables, some in rows, others interplanted more randomly with flowers, may not appeal, but breaking up the usual solid blocks may actually assist with pest control.

Mixing vegetables, herbs and flowers, will make your vegetable plot full of surprises, and interesting too.

ORNAMENTAL VEGETABLES

- Where space is really restricted, and there is insufficient room for a vegetable garden, or it is inadequate for the amount that you wish to grow, try growing some of the more decorative vegetables among the flowers.

- This has drawbacks of course – there may be gaps once harvesting time arrives. This may not be a problem if you use the vegetables as gap fillers though, and the surrounding plants grow to fill the space left after harvesting.

- Beetroot, carrots and rhubarb chard are all decorative foliage plants. Use them to help to fill in gaps in beds and borders, but don't forget that you still have to thin them, even though they are grown in clusters or groups rather than rows.

- Lettuces can be attractive until they run to seed, especially red varieties. The best ones to use are the "cut-and-come again", oak-leaf types because you can harvest the leaves without destroying the whole plant and leaving a gap.

Boundaries

Hedges, fences and walls are often overlooked at the garden-planning stage. It is tempting to see them simply as boundary markers within which the garden proper is arranged. Often it is only when the garden is complete and the boundary lowers the standard of the whole garden, that its importance is realized. A rotting fence or an ugly and overgrown hedge will mar the garden it borders, and it is much easier to consider the boundary at the design stage than it is to modify it when construction is complete.

Low walls are very practical as boundaries, and generally require much less maintenance than fences and hedges, but they often fail visually because they are too low to support most climbers and wall shrubs. Walls with a planting cavity at the top offer scope for colour and interest, but the photograph on the opposite page (below) shows how planting can be taken a step farther by providing a planting trough towards the bottom.

If you don't want to go to the trouble and expense of making a tiered wall, a similar effect can be achieved by planting slightly taller plants directly into the ground. Bear in mind, however, that plants used within the wall or at the bottom must receive regular watering. The soil at the bottom of a wall is often much drier than it is some distance away because of the rain shadow effect.

Fences, too, make good boundaries but some are more elegant than others. If well maintained, white-painted picket is one of the most attractive. This is not the first choice if privacy and security is required – when a more practical but less appealing closeboard or solid panel fence might be a better option – but in a setting with plenty of greenery and the protection of shrubs beyond the garden, it can be ideal.

Traditionally, picket fences are made from wood, but there are plastic versions if you prefer a wipe-down finish.

Many flowering shrubs can be clipped into hedges, though pruning must be done with care to avoid cutting away next year's flowers. They are also best left informal rather than clipped too rigidly. This is Spiraea x arguta.

If you have a functional but unattractive boundary fence or wall, you can hide it with shrubs, which then become the effective boundary from the visual viewpoint. In a small garden like this one, the skill lies in choosing shrubs that will grow to the height of the true boundary to mask it, without growing much larger – otherwise they can appear oppressive. Most shrubs tolerate regular pruning to keep them within bounds, however, so height and spread can usually be controlled by regular use of the pruners.

In this town garden, the boundary has, in effect, become the garden – and what lies within it is the "human area," which is cosily protected as well as stylish in appearance.

Left: *A planting trough has been added to this low wall on the road side so that passers-by derive most of the pleasure, but the same technique can be used on the garden side, too.*

Above: *The use of white-painted garden furniture with a white picket fence helps to make a garden look more serene, designed and coordinated.*

Garden illusions

The French call it *trompe l'oeil*, and deceiving the eye is an illusion a garden designer often has to adopt to make the most of an unpromising site. The few simple forms of visual deception described here should enable you to make your garden look larger than it really is or help to distract the eye from the unattractive features by making the most of the positive.

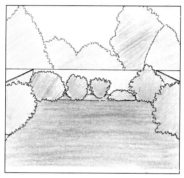

If the boundary is clearly visible, and especially if plain and man-made like a fence or a wall, a small garden will seem box-like and the boundary will dominate. Simply adding a narrow border with masking shrubs will not help because the boundary, although better clothed, will still be obvious.

By bringing the border into the garden in broad sweeps, with a hint of the lawn disappearing behind a sweep towards the end of the garden, the boundaries will be blurred and there will be the illusion of more garden beyond.

Straight lines can be uncompromising, and a dominant feature at the end of a straight path will foreshorten the visual appearance. By curving the path slightly, and perhaps tapering it slightly towards the end, there will be the illusion of greater depth. If the focal point is also diminished in height or stature, the optical illusion will be increased.

A long, straight path will take the eye to the boundary unless the garden is very large, so try to introduce a feature that will arrest the eye part way along the path. A curve around an ornament, a large shrub or small tree, will keep the eye within the garden. If you do not want to move an existing path, try erecting an arch over it, with an attractive climber to soften the outline and perhaps extended along a length of trellis on either side.

Right: *Apart from its obvious role, some colours have the visual effect of making things seem nearer or more distant, dominant or receding. This yellow* Acer japonicum *'Aureum' brings the eye to rest within the garden rather than at the garden wall or beyond. In turn, it takes the eye to the attractive stone table that might otherwise go unnoticed from a distance as its tones blend so well with the background.*

If your garden is small, and your neighbour's is attractive, leave a space between the borders and bridge the gap with an inconspicuous type of fence. The eye will then go beyond the fence, especially if there is a bold plant or tree in the distance, and create the illusion that your own garden extends much further than it actually does.

Mirrors can be used to create great illusions, and can be invaluable in making a small area look larger than it really is. A mirror placed in the frame of a disused gate – or in a false frame – will give the illusion that there is more garden beyond the door or gateway.

The combination of mirror and water, one reflected in the other, can have a dramatic effect, as this photograph shows.

Consult a mirror supplier before installing one in your garden, and explain what it is required for. You should be able to have one made to the required size if you measure up carefully first.

The illusion is soon shattered if you allow the glass to become dirty, so be prepared to keep the mirror really clean.

Focal points

Focal points are an essential part of good garden design, relevant whatever the size of garden. They help to take the eye to a favourable part and away from the less favourable. They can act as signposts to lead the eye around the garden.

Even a well-kept lawn will look bare and a little boring if it's large and all the interest is in beds and borders around the edges. It can be useful to create a focal point within the lawn, but this often works better if offset to one side or towards the end of the lawn, rather than in the centre. Position it where you want to take the eye to an attractive view, or use it to fill an area that lacks interest. Try to avoid placing the focal point against a background that is already interesting or colourful; otherwise one will fight with the other for attention.

A sundial is a popular choice, but is best placed in a sunny position if it is to look in the least credible. A birdbath is another popular choice, especially if it is close to the house where the birds can be seen and enjoyed.

Above: *Gateways and arches make excellent focal points, and if used to divide a large garden can add a sense of mystery and promise from whichever side you view. This device works best if the areas either side are in contrasting styles or are visually very different. The garden on one side of this wall is heavily planted and enclosed, whereas the view beyond suggests open lawns and spaciousness.*

In a long, narrow garden, you could produce a series of arches or gates, each taking the eye and the mind further on into a journey of exploration.

Left: *Focal points can be plants as well as inanimate objects. When the two are used together, the effect can be particularly striking.*

In this large garden, the old mature hedges produce a predominantly green effect: restful but visually uninspiring. A statue has transformed an unexciting view into an arresting scene that demands attention. But foreground plants are important too and, if large, can help to put the rest of the garden into more reasonable proportions. These bold red hot pokers (Kniphofia) have the height to counterbalance the statue, and their strong colour accentuates the effect.

In a small garden it can be a good idea to have the sitting area away from the house so that there appears to be a larger area of interest between home and boundary. In this attractive scene, the white chairs provide the necessary contrast and height to act as a focal point. This kind of focal point only works well, however, if the background is attractive – avoid taking the eye towards a tatty old fence.

A tall, narrow object such as a bird-bath or sundial on a plinth needs added visual impact from a distance, and setting it on a bold base like this gravelled area edged with bricks is one way to achieve this.

In a small garden, a spectacular focal point can be used to dominate a corner of the garden so that the limitations of scale and size become irrelevant for the moment. A well-placed ornament or figure will serve as a simple focal point. In this garden, the white trellis that frames the statue helps to fill this particular corner, and immediately creates the impression of style and elegance.

Solutions for shade

Shady gardens are a challenge. The emphasis will have to be on foliage rather than bright flowers unless you are prepared to keep replanting with short-term seasonal plants. By using shade-tolerant plants and techniques to make the most of available light, however, shady gardens can have a strong sense of design and a charm and elegance lacking in sunny gardens.

You will find a list of dependable shade plants on page 86, though of course, there are hundreds more that are widely available from garden centres and mail-order nurseries.

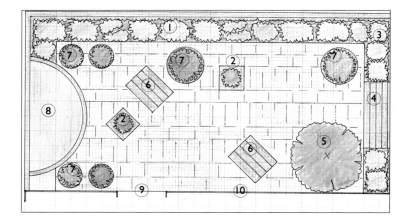

1	Raised bed	6	Chair
2	Table with plant in container	7	Hostas or other shade plants in pots
3	Walls with climbers	8	Raised pond
4	Garden bench	9	Door
5	Japanese maple or other small tree in tub	10	House

Every garden has some shady areas: this is inevitable where there are buildings, hedges or walls, and tall trees. The problem is usually at its worst, however, in small enclosed gardens with high walls, typically found in basement areas. There will be parts that the sun probably never reaches, and the whole area is likely to suffer from low light levels. The simple design shown above right is one solution to this difficult problem, and despite its simplicity and small size incorporates many elements that can be adopted for shady gardens large and small.

Raised beds not only add a touch of interest to what would otherwise be a box-like flat area, they also bring the plants a little nearer to the light. Generally, this will have little benefit, but in some parts of the garden it will be sufficient to bring a touch of direct sun for an hour or two.

Climbers have been used to clothe the walls, which will in turn make them look less oppressive, but they must be kept well pruned back to prevent them overhanging the garden and creating even more shade.

Plants in pots and tubs give added flexibility. With a design as limited as this, you want to be able to move things around occasionally, just as you might want to rearrange the furniture in a room from time to time.

The garden bench at one end is positioned to give the longest possible view to the raised pond, which is in any case the focal point of the garden. The sight and sound of water is an invaluable attribute in a shady garden. You will not be able to grow sun-lovers such as waterlilies successfully, but there are shade-tolerant water plants, and water can be successful simply as a surface texture even without plants growing in it.

Small gardens enclosed by high walls usually have an acute shade problem, but they can still be successful, provided mainly shade-tolerant plants are used, with the emphasis on foliage plants.

It is important to reflect as much light as possible. The area will look less gloomy, and the plants will derive some benefit from the reflected light. So use pale paving rather than a dark colour or clay bricks or pavers, and be generous with the white paint. It will make the area look more attractive, and its reflective qualities will make the whole area appear lighter.

Right: *Even in "normal" gardens with areas bathed in sunlight for much of the day, there will be gloomy areas. Fences, walls and hedges may be more of a problem than trees: although the shadows are usually shorter because their height is less, their length means that there is less chance of the sun moving around the obstruction. One side of a boundary or wall can be in shade for most of the day.*

Here the focal points should be light and bold to offset their dull background. Try painting a white circle on a fence or wall in permanent gloom, then set your focal point in this. Use a succession of seasonal plants grown to flowering stage in good light, like the camassia and hippeastrum in this picture. Sometimes the angle of the light is sufficient to highlight the flowers for part of the day if placed a little forward of the fence or wall.

If you do not want to use paint in case you decide to change your mind, cut out a circular piece of wood, paint it white, and nail or screw that to the background.

Left: *The garden floor can have a dramatic effect on how inviting or gloomy a shady part of the garden looks. Light and bright paths will make the area look interesting, even if the plants lack colour. Pale gravel or paving slabs will both make a feature of the path in a low-light area. In this example, beach pebbles have also been used imaginatively to create a simple focal point and again lighten the dark background.*

Screens and disguises

Unless you are extremely fortunate, there will be a view or objects within the garden that you want to hide. Focal points can be used to take the eye away from some of them, but others will require some form of screening or disguise.

Many common hedging plants can be allowed to grow taller than normal to form a shrubby screen. Space the plants further apart than for a hedge, so that they retain a shrubby shape, and clip or prune only when it is necessary to keep within bounds. Avoid a formal, clipped shape unless you are screening within a very formal garden. Most hedging plants will grow to twice their normal hedge height if you give them more space and do not restrict them by frequent clipping and pruning.

Choose plants appropriate to the setting. In a Japanese-style garden, many of the tall bamboos will make an excellent screen for, say, a garage wall or oil storage tank. Use shrubby plants in a garden where there are lots of shrubs, and especially if the shrub border can be taken up to the screening point. On a patio, a climber-covered trellis may look more appropriate.

In town gardens, and especially in the case of balcony and roof gardens, the problem is to minimize the impact of surrounding homes, offices and factories. These usually require impracticably huge walls to mask the view, which would also make the garden excessively dark. In a very small garden, trees may not be a practical solution for this type of screening either, although in a large one they will probably provide the answer.

A sensible compromise is to extend the wall or fence with a trellis, or similar framework, along which you can grow climbers. This will not block out the view completely, but it will soften the harsh impact of buildings and help to concentrate the eye within the garden by minimizing the distractions beyond. The boundary itself will be given extra height and interest.

A combination of plants and hard landscaping is often the most pleasing way to screen a view beyond a boundary. Trees are a particularly pleasing solution. Even if they lose their leaves in winter, the network of branches is often sufficient to break up the harsh outline of buildings beyond, and in summer – when you are in the garden and require more privacy – the canopy of foliage will usually block out most of the view beyond. Trees are a particularly good solution if the aspect is such that most of the shadow falls away from your garden rather than over it.

A painted trellis makes an attractive and easily erected screen, and if you make it tall enough and use it to form an L-shaped corner where you can create a cosy sitting area, the screen can become an attractive feature in its own right. The secret of stylish screening is to turn it into a positive feature whenever possible. If you give it a purpose, it will be less obviously a screen intended to hide something and become a positive part of your garden.

Left: *Using bright flowers or interesting focal points within a garden concentrates the eye on the positive points and not the negative surrounding ones.*

Above: *In this garden, an arbour has been created that provides height and privacy, with climbers over the top adding even more screening.*

The strong formal design, with a circle at its centre, also uses a design technique that takes the eye inwards rather than outwards to what lies beyond the boundary. This clever use of clay pavers shows a circular centrepiece laid to an angled herringbone pattern, with basket-weave used for the rectangular areas of paving.

Improving dull spots and corners

One of the skills of good garden design is not to waste any available space. Even those unpromising, problem positions between houses; awkwardly shaped spots and corners that do not seem to fit easily into the main design; dry and shady areas beneath trees and shrubs where nothing seems to thrive, and anywhere that looks bare or uninteresting should be exploited, and planted whenever possible.

Bare ground – or steps – in a dull spot can often be transformed by the simple addition of an ornament or a group of containers. But try to make it a little special: choose different shapes and sizes of containers, and a range of flowering and foliage plants. If the dull corner is in a flowerbed, try using a broken urn or pot set on its side with soil covering the rim, then plant a widening and winding "flow" of low-growing and long-flowering bedding plants such as pansies, so that it appears as if the plants are pouring out from the tilted container.

Ornaments and statues can be used in a similar way, but they should be light in colour to contrast with a dark background.

Statues can look incongruous in the wrong setting, but superb in a style of garden that is appropriate. They look best in traditional country-garden styles with lots of shrubs and flower borders. If you can set them with plants around the base they will look less pretentious and appear to be a more integrated part of the overall garden design.

In a very unpromising corner, be content with an attractive statue, and a tough climber like ivy planted against the wall (choose a gold-variegated variety to lighten the area). Interesting paving also helps, so try mixing paving materials, or perhaps create pebbled areas on which to stand the containers.

Corners where fences meet can be particularly difficult to brighten up, especially if they are in a shady position. This corner previously had grass almost to the edge of the fence with just a narrow ribbon border. It has been transformed by taking a large sweep out of the lawn and filling the area with a coloured gravel on which to frame a collection of plants in containers. This simple device can be used in most gardens to transform an otherwise dull and uninteresting corner into an eye-catching feature.

The shady side of a hedge can be a particular problem, as few flowering plants will thrive in dry shade. An attractive container at the end of a path or in a corner of the lawn or flowerbeds where nothing much grows will act as a focal point; and bring a touch of much-needed lightness if pale flowers and foliage are used.

A container raised on a plinth will generally be more successful in design terms than one at ground level. It will make more of a feature and the additional height may bring the plants into better light. White or pale-coloured flowers and pale foliage plants can look particularly stunning against a dark background such as a conifer hedge.

Water features

Water plays an important part in most good garden design, and if you look at the work of many professional garden designers you will find water somewhere. Not everyone wants a pond, of course, especially if safety is a concern where there are young children, but there are lots of water features where the risk is minimal while still creating maximum impact as a focal point. Whether or not you include a pond, try to find space for a simple water feature such as a wall or pebble fountain.

Wall fountains are a good choice for a formal garden or a patio, although they can also be used with great effect in an informal setting too. Lion faces and gargoyles look perfectly in place in a period garden.

You can buy suitable wall masks complete as a kit with pump. If you don't want a small pool at the bottom like the one in the photograph on the opposite page, buy an integrated wall fountain that includes a shallow dish that fixes to the wall along with the spout. This can be positioned beyond the reach of small children, and in any case the basins contain very little water.

Only a small pump is required, and many can be powered by a simple low-voltage system. The mains power is reduced by a transformer indoors so that only a low-voltage cable is required outdoors.

A wall fountain is usually fitted by drilling and plugging the wall so that it can be screwed into position. The difficult part is disguising the pipe between the submerged pump and the wall spout. The pipe is best hidden within the brickwork when the wall is constructed, but often this is not possible. You may be able to remove a channel in the brickwork, but the pipework will still be visible unless you camouflage it. The simplest way to fix the pipe to an existing wall is to clamp it to the face of the brick and then plant ivy or some other evergreen climber to cover it. After a year or two, the pipe probably won't be visible from a distance.

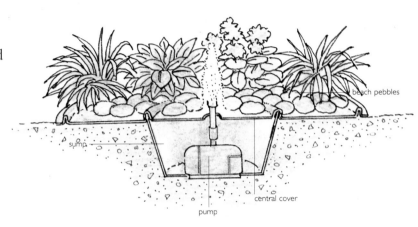

Above: *Simple fountains like this can be bought complete with reservoir and pump. Making this pebble fountain can take just one day.*

MAKING A PEBBLE POOL

1 For any bubble fountain or pebble pool you will need a reservoir, or sump, to house the pump and hold a generous reserve of water. Proprietary products are by far the easiest to install as they are designed with a wide rim to catch water that has drifted, with a centrepiece to support the pebbles over the reservoir. Some garden centres stock these, or you can order them from water garden specialists.

   Make sure the reservoir is well supported, removing or adding more soil as necessary. If the soil is very stony, bed on a layer of sand. Make sure it is level, with the rim at or just below the surrounding paving or soil. If surrounded by soil, positioning the lip slightly above bed level will reduce the amount of soil contaminating the fountain.

2 Insert the pump and take the wire out at a side where it can be hidden easily as it emerges from the wide rim. If there is paving on one side and a flowerbed on the other, take it out on the flowerbed side so that it can easily be camouflaged.

3 Insert the central cover, then add the beach pebbles. You can buy these from some garden centres, otherwise obtain them from a stone merchant or builder's merchant.

4 Fill with water and turn on the pump. Installing a spectacular water feature like this is that simple.

Above: *It is always a good idea to have plenty of plants growing around a wall fountain, otherwise attention will drawn to what could be an expanse of plain brickwork.*

Right: *Rock gardens and streams with cascades are a natural choice for a sloping site, and they can often be combined. If the slope is gentle, the design could be mainly lawn with rock and water features as the main theme of the garden.*

Left: *Simple but effective water features can be built for little cost. This one has been made from an old dustbin lid! The lid is supported over a reservoir that also contains a small low-voltage pump, and beach pebbles have been used to give the feature more interest and character. The water simply flows over the rim and into the reservoir to be recirculated.*

The reservoir can be made from the base of a cut-down dustbin, or a waterproof container (you can even just use an excavation in the ground and line it with a waterproof pond liner). Some water is lost regularly through evaporation and splashes that drift in the wind. So if you cannot see the water level in the reservoir, make a point of topping it up every few days (simply pour more water into the basin or over the stones – if the reservoir is full, it will overflow into the surrounding ground).

Using furniture

A garden without furniture implies a garden that is all work and no play. Furniture creates the impression of a garden designed to be used for relaxation, a place to rest and enjoy the fruit of earlier labours. It has to be used with care, however, as the choice of material and the style of furniture can look incongruous if it does not reflect the mood of the rest of the garden. Some furniture is purely functional, while other pieces can be as important a focal point as a well-chosen ornament.

Furniture can become the feature of a paved area, especially if it lacks a natural focal point. Although the garden featured on the right immediately generates a pleasant atmosphere, any clear-cut lines that relate to an overall plan are obscured by the difficult site. In an area heavily shaded by trees, the paving gives the illusion of an area in a forest clearing, with dappled light filtering through. Without the containers and the furniture, this kind of area could lack visual stimulation and look rather barren. The lavish use of plants in containers gives it colour and texture, but it is the furniture that draws the eye and holds the area together.

Tree seats have a special charm, and are often useful as a focal point in a part of the garden otherwise lacking interest, such as areas of grass with large trees and little else. If painted white, a tree seat will stand out across the garden, and is sure to add a touch of elegance.

Tree seats are more use as a focal point and garden ornament than as practical seats, however, as the white paint soon looks grubby and unpleasant unless you wipe it down regularly, and drips, midges and falling leaves are always a risk if you sit beneath the overhanging branches of a tree.

In this setting, white plastic or resin furniture would sit uneasily, but wood blends with the paving and the woodland effect of the setting. Cushions – which must be taken inside when not in use – add another dash of restrained colour, and will help to offset the rather austere appearance that some wooden furniture often has.

Use an attractive garden seat to liven up an otherwise dull area of the garden, perhaps where mainly green shrubs or a dark hedge forms a backdrop to the lawn. As these pictures show, a scene that is rather mundane and uninteresting can be transformed by the simple addition of a garden seat. It also invites you to walk over to it, and to use a part of the garden that may not otherwise hold special appeal.

BUILT-IN FURNITURE

Built-in furniture is a sensible option for a patio where space is limited. If you have plenty of space, free-standing furniture is much more adaptable, and by rearranging it you can add variety. In a small area, however, built-in seats and a barbecue can give your patio a very "designed" appearance. You will still require supplementary free-standing furniture of course, but less of it.

Barbecues and wooden seats are commonly integrated into the walls created as part of the patio boundary, but if you have a raised bed around the edge, a simple sitting area like the one illustrated below will give that special feeling that you get when surrounded by plants. Bear in mind, of course, that when certain plants are in flower, like this geranium, bees and wasps may be a problem.

Above: *Tree seats almost always have to be made to measure and adapted to suit the diameter of the tree – or in this case the area occupied by multiple trunks – which gives great scope for that touch of individuality in design.*

Left: *Built-in seats can be very straightforward to create, like this concrete "seat".*

The magic of ornaments

Ornaments should be used around the garden just as they are in the home. Use them simply to display their inherent beauty, to brighten up otherwise uninspiring areas, to make a statement about taste or style, and as punctuation points that form part of the garden decor.

Small ornaments can be moved around, so they are also a means of making subtle changes of emphasis over time. You may want to use them as a focal point in one part of the garden in winter, and in another in summer.

Shrub borders can become tired-looking and a trifle boring when there are no flowers, but a well-placed ornament can transform the ordinary into something special. The ornament can easily be moved to different positions as different parts of the border or garden need a little uplift.

Ornaments and figures are frequently placed in a prominent position, such as on a plinth at the end of a path or vista, in an alcove, or in a conspicuous open area such as a lawn or area of paving. Sometimes, however, a more subtle approach can be particularly pleasing, and placing an ornament within a flowerbed is often very successful.

This figure is subtle rather than bold, and set in a flowerbed it does not make a strong focal point across the garden. But if you choose an ornament because of its pleasing appearance, this may be the best way to view it, as it is in harmony with its surroundings. Just as a painting in a gallery is not necessarily positioned as a focal point but in a way that shows it to advantage, so the placing of an interesting ornament can be done in a similar way.

Ornaments often come into their own in winter, when much of the garden is drab and lacks colour or impact. A dusting of snow can actually enhance them.

Japanese gardeners use ornaments symbolically, and lanterns like this one have particular purposes and meanings, but they can be used anywhere that pleases you, whether or not the garden is in a Japanese style. This lantern has been used to add interest to a rather dull part of a conifer bed, which is mulched with a layer of gravel.

A good garden designer always keeps an eye open for suitable materials with which to create statements or focal points. A natural material, like a piece of rock, can be as beautiful and attention-grabbing as any abstract man-made ornament. These four stones look almost casual in their positioning, but they have been selected and positioned with great care. In fact, they are more likely to be the subject of admiring glances than the striking plants around them.

Grouping containers

Groups of containers are almost always more pleasing than single pots dotted around in isolation, especially if they are ordinary pots or mediocre containers. You can hide quite ordinary containers behind smaller but more attractive ones by using a stepped effect, with the taller plants in bigger pots behind.

PLANTING A TUB OR URN

1 Even when containers are to be grouped, it is wise to include some mixed plantings instead of a separate pot for each plant. For these, choose a large pot or other container, and make sure there is a drainage layer of broken clay pots or something like coarsely chipped bark at the bottom.

2 Fill with a good quality potting soil. For seasonal plants a peat-based or peat-substitute compost will be satisfactory provided you feed frequently, but for shrubby plants or perennials, a loam-based potting soil is preferable. It will still require feeding, but the plants will be less prone to starvation.

Start with a tall plant in the centre, always firming it in and making sure the top of the root-ball is covered with a good layer of potting soil.

3 Fill in with more plants around the edge to give the container a well-clothed look, but avoid trailers that will completely obscure an attractive pot like this, which deserves to be seen.

4 If the pot or container is attractive in its own right, make the most of it. Use mainly upright plants and position the container so that it is in a dominant position within the group.

Sometimes choosing a group of containers with contrasting shapes and sizes can work, especially if they are used to add height and perhaps to fill in a visually bare area.

However you arrange your containers, they should have a sense of harmony. Even if the plants are very different – and this group includes shrubs, succulents, bedding plants and border perennials – the use of decorative terracotta containers holds the collection together and gives the group a sense of unity.

Pots are usually grouped on a patio or paved area, and can transform an otherwise dull corner. The individual plants in this group of containers are unspectacular, but when displayed as a feature collectively they are just as attractive as a flowerbed. For groups in such a prominent position, however, it is necessary to rotate containers periodically so that there is always something interesting or seasonal to be seen. Unless you move a plant that has passed its best, it will mar the rest of the group.

Focus on containers

If a plant is spectacular or a container interesting or eye-catching, it is best to display it in isolation rather than in a group of plants or pots. Use it as a focal point to take the eye to a particular part of the garden. Or use them formally to flank a front door or guard a flight of steps.

Do not cover a spectacular container with trailing plants. Use upright plants that make the most of the container itself.

Garden objects from watering-cans to wheelbarrows make interesting containers. In a modern garden you can use modern objects, but in a country garden or one created in a rural or old-fashioned style, an old container will be more appropriate.

This old wooden wheelbarrow has long since been replaced by a lighter modern version, but with a coat of bright paint and a few drainage holes made in the base it will see many more years of eye-catching service.

Everyday objects such as old paint tins (though nowadays they are usually plastic) can be pressed into use with a little imagination. They will give your patio or garden that individual touch that bought containers simply cannot achieve. These two old paint containers have been painted white first, then had coloured "drips" added to match the colour of the gerberas.

Always make drainage holes in the base of containers that do not already have them before you plant them up.

There are some places where flowers will fail to thrive, but if the container is striking enough, you will not need them. The shrub border in this picture was uninspiring before the addition of this large empty jar, which has transformed the area into one of great interest.

Above: *If both plant and container are big and bold, they do not have to be colourful or spectacular. This* Fatsia japonica *brings instant appeal to a shady part of the garden that would otherwise lack any points of interest.*

Left: *If the container is striking enough, the flowers can be almost incidental. In fact, a very bold floral display may actually detract from a spectacular or unusual container.*

The container illustrated is eye-catching in both shape and colour, and in its own way challenges the flowers to compete. This kind of container commands attention and takes the eye to that part of the garden. Avoid too many containers like this in close proximity, however, as they will vie for attention and the impact will be lessened.

Lighting

Enjoyment of your garden should not cease at sundown. Garden lighting will enable you to sit outside on warm evenings when you can see your garden in a new light, and in the cold dark days of winter you can enjoy spectacular effects from indoors.

Do not be afraid to try garden lighting just because electricity is potentially dangerous. There are lots of excellent low-voltage systems that should remove the worry, and for mains voltage consult your local qualified electrician for assistance.

In small town gardens, roof gardens and on balconies, floodlights and spotlights of the kind that can be so effective in a large garden may be inappropriate. Glaring lights may annoy neighbours, so more subtle lighting is usually more suitable. Small lanterns, and low-voltage lights that cast their beam downwards or over just a small area, are unlikely to offend anyone. The use of some stronger patio lighting will be necessary, however, for an area that you are going to use in the evening. Just make sure most of the beam is focused towards the ground, which is where it is needed for safety.

For lighting to be a permanent feature, electric lighting is the practical option, but candles and flares can be used for the odd occasion when you want to invite your friends around for an evening out with a difference, a true candlelight dinner perhaps. Patio flares burn quite brightly, and lanterns are available that will protect candles from the wind and cast a reasonably localized light. Candles are for "atmospheric" light, however, and are really only practical where there is some supplementary light from a nearby electric lamp, from the house for instance.

Garden lighting can also be used to create focal points after dark, but the spotlights for this are best installed during construction to avoid the problem of laying cables across or around paved and heavily planted areas. Ideally, several lighting points should be wired in at this stage, giving you plenty of flexibility later so that the lights can be moved around to make the most of seasonal variations.

Spotlights should be unobtrusive by day – preferably well hidden among some plants. Upward-pointing beams can be very striking and effective, but it is best to avoid them if the beams are likely to be thrown into your neighbours' windows.

INSTALLING LOW-VOLTAGE LIGHTING

1 Low-voltage lighting is simple to install, and usually comes in a kit with everything you need. Always follow the manufacturer's instructions on the kit, and ask a qualified electrician to follow the rest of these instructions.

2 Drill a hole in the wall or window frame to pass the low-voltage cable through. Remember to fill the hole with mastic to produce a waterproof seal around the cable.

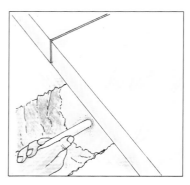

4 You should have a choice of designs for the lights, so choose those that are appropriate to the style of the garden and their position. A kit usually includes several lights, which are easy to fix and reposition if you follow the manufacturer's instructions.

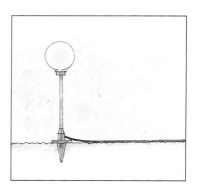

3 Whenever possible, take the cable underground. Electrically, it is not a hazard to life because of the low voltage it carries, but trailing cables are a hazard as you may trip over them. Paths are a special problem, and the cable should be passed under them whenever possible. Excavate an area on either side, undercutting the path a little, and then push through a piece of conduit. Thread the cable through the conduit.

Spotlights are often used to pick out ornaments or striking structural features, but bold plants such as red hot pokers (Kniphofia) and yuccas make good focal points at night. In this picture fennel takes centre stage.

In this beautiful garden, the decorative lighting has been confined to chains of small lights draped through the tree, and to a small lantern. Light from the house, or supplementary lighting, is turned on when the area is used for sitting out in the evening during the summer.

Flares and candlelight contribute enormously to the atmosphere when you are relaxing outside in the evening.

Paths and paving

Paths and areas of paving such as patios give the garden its backbone and shape. While seasonal plants are momentarily spectacular, they come and go, but the hard surfacing remains as a year-round reminder of the basic garden design, and will show up its strengths and weaknesses. It is worth spending time, thought and money on getting the framework of paths and paving right.

Concrete paving blocks remain a popular choice because they are readily available in a wide range of finishes and are much cheaper than natural stone alternatives. The formal and regular shape needs to be offset by lavish planting that spills over the edges to create a soft, well-clothed look. A neutral colour is often more successful than a mixture of bright colours (which soon become uniformly dull anyway with age). Small sizes usually look best in a small area, and are easier to handle and lay.

LAYING BRICKS AND CLAY PAVERS

1 If a path will have to take heavy use, bed bricks on mortar, but for paths only subject to occasional foot traffic you can bed them on sand, like clay pavers. In either case, prepare a sound and stable sub-base.

2 Lay several rows of bricks, then tap them flat using a mallet or the handle of a club hammer over a straight-edged piece of wood. On a narrow path you will not need to build in a slight fall, but on a large area such as for a patio, this will be necessary to ensure water drains away freely.

3 The easiest way to mortar the joints between bricks is to brush in a dry mix, pressing it down between the bricks with a small piece of wood to eliminate large air pockets.

4 Finally, spray with water from a compression sprayer or a watering-can fitted with a fine rose. Apply just enough water to clean the surface of the bricks and moisten between the joints. If necessary, clean off any mortar stains with a damp cloth before they dry.

In parts of the garden where the path is not subject to regular heavy use, a more random appearance can be very effective, and if you allow a few suitable plants to meander between and around the paving the effect can be very pleasing.

Even in a small area, mixing materials and providing strong lines will create a positive impression of imaginative design. In this garden, the main surfacing materials are concrete paving slabs and gravel, but they have been separated by old railway sleepers that add a contrast of texture and colour. A garden area like this will remain attractive even when the summer plants have died down.

Even small paths leading to odd corners of the garden deserve careful thought. This short path that leads from the main garden to a wooden seat has been made into a feature as strong as the borders that flank it or the seat that it leads to. If only rectangular paving slabs had been used it would have been unremarkable and uninteresting, but the addition of a few patterned pavers and pebbles has managed to transform it into a distinctive path packed with interest.

Most of this book has been about the principles of planning the hard landscaping, using focal points, and making the most of difficult areas by clever design techniques. It is impossible to give many planting suggestions for beds and borders in a book of this size, and in any case you should try to include mainly those plants that appeal to you rather than follow another person's preferences. Most garden centres now have well-labelled plants, often with a picture of the mature plant as well as notes about its height, spread, soil preferences and what sort of aspect it prefers, and a good plant encyclopedia will fill in most of the gaps.

The vast majority of plants will grow well in most gardens, tolerating a wide pH range (a measure of how acid or alkaline the soil is), and doing well in sun or partial shade. It is only where your soil is extreme in some way, or the aspect particularly unfavourable (very shady, exposed and windy, or very acid or alkaline, for example), that you will have to consider whether the plant will thrive.

This section of the book tells you which plants should be suitable for a range of problem sites, so you know which ones to consider when you browse through catalogues or go around the garden centres.

There are also suggestions for other groups of plants for which ideas are usually welcome, such as those that make a good focal point, and plants to grow for wildlife, or for fragrance.

Bear in mind that these short lists are only a selection of the many plants that may be appropriate. But they are all dependable plants, and are well worth including as, at least, a starting point.

Focal point plants

The majority of these plants look good in borders, but most of them are particularly striking as individual specimens, or in a position where they stand out above the rest of the plants in the border. They are plants that will catch the eye, even from a distance, and in many cases serve a similar purpose to a garden ornament.

BORDER PERENNIALS

Acanthus spinosus (bears breeches)
Above: Large, divided, spiny-looking leaves, topped by 1.2m (4ft) spikes of unusual purple and white flowers in summer.

Agapanthus hybrids (African lily)
Above: Large, rounded heads of blue flowers on stiff stems about 60–75cm (2–2½ft) tall, make an excellent focal point when grown in a large container.

Allium giganteum (giant onion) Ball-like heads about 10cm (4in) across containing masses of small, mauve flowers on stiff stems about 1.2m (4ft) tall.

Crambe cordifolia (colewort)
Above: Huge, dark green leaves and cloud-like masses of small, white flowers in early summer on stems about 1.8m (6ft) tall.

Eremurus robustus (foxtail lily)
Above: Tall, rocket-like flower spikes often 2.4m (8ft) tall in late spring and early summer. This species has peach-coloured flowers.

Gunnera manicata
Enormous leaves like a giant rhubarb, on plants up to 3m (10ft) tall. It requires very moist soil.

Kniphofia (red hot poker)
Above: Stiff, blade-like leaves and poker-like spikes of usually red and yellow flowers, 1–1.8m (3–6ft) tall.

Phormium tenax (New Zealand flax)
Above: Clumps of broad strap-like leaves, green, purple or variegated, according to species or variety; most are 1–1.8m (3–6ft) tall.

GRASSES

Arundo donax
A large grass, up to 2.4m (8ft) with long, drooping, blue-green leaves. 'Variegatus', banded white, is only about half this height.

Cortaderia selloana (pampas grass)
Above: Large grass with 1.8m (6ft) long, silvery white flower plumes in autumn. Evergreen. For a small garden use 'Pumila' – 1.2m (4ft).

SHRUBS AND TREES

Cordyline australis (cabbage palm)
Above: Palm that is hardy except in cold areas. Strap-shaped leaves (on tall stems on mature plants). Can reach tree-like size.

Fatsia japonica (false castor oil plant)
Above: Hand-shaped, large, glossy green leaves. White, ball-shaped flower head in autumn on mature plants. 1.8m (6ft) or more tall.

Garrya elliptica (silk tassel bush)
Evergreen of undistinguished appearance most of year, but spectacular long catkins in winter.

Mahonia 'Charity'
Evergreen with stiff, upright growth and large, divided leaves. Sprays of yellow flowers in winter. Grows up to 2.4m (8ft) or more.

Paulownia tomentosa (coppiced)
If pruned to just above ground level each spring, this tree can be grown as a tall shrub with leaves 60cm (2ft) or more across.

Trachycarpus fortunei (Chusan palm)
Above: Clusters of large, fan-shaped leaves on a tall stem. Only hardy in areas where winters are mild.

Yucca gloriosa (and *Y. filamentosa*)
Above: Stiff, sword-like evergreen leaves (on a stout stem in the case of *Y. gloriosa*), with imposing spike of creamy-white bells.

Plants for shady areas

Shade-tolerant plants are among the most useful in the garden as they can make the most of those unpromising areas that are usually dull and uninteresting. A few well-chosen, attractive shade plants can transform those parts of the garden that receive little direct sun into a lush and lovely area that you will not want to avoid.

BORDER PERENNIALS FOR DRY SHADE

Anemone japonica (*A.* x *hybrida*)
White or pink, single or double flowers about 5cm (2in) across in late summer and autumn, on stems 1–1.2m (3–4ft) tall.

Bergenia (elephant ears)
Above: Large, rounded, glossy leathery leaves (sometimes purplish in winter). Flowers – mostly pink – in spring. 30–45cm (1–1½ft).

Brunnera macrophylla
Loose heads of blue, forget-me-not-like flowers in spring, but taller at about 45cm (1½ft). Avoid dry soil.

Euphorbia (spurge)
There are many kinds, but for shade look for *E. amygdaloides*, *E. griffithii* and *E. robbiae* (one of the best for shade).

Liriope muscari (lilyturf)
Grass-like tufts of foliage, with spikes of blue, bead-like flowers in autumn. 30–45cm (1–1½ft).

Pulmonaria (lungwort)
There are many species and varieties, most with silver-splashed leaves. The spring flowers are in shades of blue and pink.

BORDER PERENNIALS FOR MOIST SHADE

Astilbe hybrids
Above: Deeply cut foliage, topped with plumes of pink, red or white summer flowers. 60–75cm (2–2½ft).

Astrantia (masterwort)
White to pink flowers with papery bracts, on slender stems, in summer. 60-75cm (2-2½ft).

Dicentra spectabilis (bleeding heart)
Fern-like foliage, topped by arching sprays of pendulous pink or white flowers in spring. 60cm (2ft).

Helleborus (hellebore)
The most popular species are *H. niger* (winter) and *H. orientalis* (spring), but there are other species and hybrids to try.

Hosta (plantain lily)
These popular foliage plants come in many variations, so choose species or varieties with leaves that particularly appeal to you.

Rodgersia
Large, bold, divided or lobed leaves (there are several species) and plumes of white or pink flowers in summer. 1–1.5m (3–5ft).

SHRUBS FOR DRY SHADE

Aucuba japonica (spotted laurel)
Above: Large, glossy evergreen leaves, splashed yellow or gold. Flowers insignificant, occasionally red berries. 1.5m (5ft).

Ilex (holly)
There are dozens of excellent hollies, many attractively variegated. If you want berries, check that you are buying a female variety.

Mahonia
There are many species and hybrids, all with large, divided leaves and yellow flowers in winter or spring.

Pachysandra terminalis
A low-growing ground cover about 30cm (1ft) tall, with white, insignificant flowers. 'Variegata' is a more attractive plant.

Skimmia
Glossy-leaved evergreens, with red berries (if you buy a female variety or one that has flowers of both sexes). About 1m (3ft).

Vinca (periwinkle)
A rather untidy, spreading ground cover, but useful for its usually blue flowers all summer long. There are variegated forms.

SHRUBS FOR MOIST SHADE

Camellia
Above: Large flowers in spring, set against glossy, evergreen leaves. There are many different kinds.

Fatsia japonica (false castor oil plant)
A bold foliage plant with large, hand-shaped leaves. Grows to about 1.8m (6ft).

Hamamelis mollis (witch hazel)
A large shrub to 3m (10ft) or more, grown for its spidery-looking, yellow, fragrant flowers in winter.

Rhododendron
Popular flowering woodland plants. There are hundreds of widely available varieties to choose from.

Sarcococca (sweet box)
Glossy, evergreen foliage and white, winter flowers that are small but very fragrant. About 1m (3ft).

Viburnum davidii
Low-growing evergreen with conspicuously veined leathery leaves. Turquoise fruits on female plants.

Plants for sunny and dry areas

Few plants object to sunshine, but the dry soil that sometimes goes with a shallow or sandy soil in a sun-baked situation is a more demanding environment. For a position like this, choose plants that are naturally adapted to such conditions and will thrive in them.

SHRUBS

Caryopteris x *clandonensis* (blue spiraea)
Clusters of bright blue flowers in late summer and early autumn. Grey, aromatic leaves. Height about 1m (3ft).

Helianthemum nummularium (rock rose)
Above: Low-growing shrubs to about 30cm (1ft), with masses of single or double pink, red, yellow or white flowers in early summer.

Cistus (rock rose)
Above: Large, single flowers between late spring and mid-summer. Mainly pinks and white, and often blotched. 45–90cm (1½–3ft).

Convolvulus cneorum
A leafy evergreen with a silvery appearance. Funnel-shaped, white flowers in summer, on a plant that grows to about 60cm (2ft).

Cytisus (broom)
There are many species and hybrids to choose from, mainly with bright, pea-type flowers.

Santolina chamaecyparissus (cotton lavender)
Finely divided, stem-hugging grey leaves that create a silvery mound about 60cm (2ft) tall. Button-like, yellow flowers in summer.

Senecio
S. greyi and *S.* 'Sunshine' *(above)* are similar plants with grey leaves on bushy plants about 1m (3ft) tall. Yellow daisy flowers in summer.

Yucca
Any of the hardy yuccas make imposing plants, with spiky leaves and bold spikes of white, bell-like flowers in summer.

BORDER PERENNIALS

Achillea filipendulina (yarrow)
Above: Flat, yellow flower heads over fern-like foliage, flowering at intervals between early summer and mid-autumn. 1.2m (4ft).

Agapanthus (African lily)
Large, rounded heads of blue flowers on stiff stems about 60–75cm (2–2½ft) tall. Not suitable for cold winter areas.

Echinops ritro (globe thistle)
Above: Globular, steely-blue flower heads in mid- and late summer, on plants about 1m (3ft) tall with grey-green, deeply lobed leaves.

Geranium (cranesbill)
Above: There are many species of these summer-flowering border plants, with pink or blue flowers, most 30–60cm (1–2ft) tall.

Iris germanica hybrids (flag)
The border flag irises, which flower in early summer, come in many colours. Most grow to about 60–90cm (2–3ft) tall.

Kniphofia hybrids (red hot poker)
Stiff, blade-like leaves and imposing poker-like spikes of usually red and yellow flowers. 1–1.8m (3–6ft) tall.

Nepeta mussinii (N. x *faassenii*) (catmint)
Above: Massed spikes of blue flowers in summer, backed by grey-green leaves. Grows up to 30–60cm (1–2ft) according to variety.

Verbascum (mullein)
There are several good hybrids for the border, but they tend to be short-lived. Tall spikes of pink, yellow or white flowers.

Plants for chalky soil

Alkaline soils – predominantly those that are in chalky areas – pose a problem for many plants. The high pH (alkalinity) can cause various nutrients and trace elements to become locked into a form unavailable to the plants, which then grow poorly and often have yellowing leaves. You can overcome some of these problems with cultural techniques and the use of special chemicals, but it is easier to concentrate on those plants that grow well on chalky soils.

SHRUBS

Buddleia davidii (butterfly bush)
Annual pruning ensures sprays of white, mauve or purple flowers on bushes about 1.8m (6ft) tall.

Clematis
Above and top: There are many species and hybrids of these popular climbers to be grown, all of which should thrive on chalky soils.

Cotoneaster
Choose from the many kinds of cotoneaster, deciduous or evergreen, ground-huggers or tall shrubs. All tolerate chalky soil.

Helianthemum nummularium (sun rose)
Low-growing shrubs to about 30cm (1ft), with masses of single or double pink, red, yellow or white flowers in early summer.

Lavandula (lavender)
Above: Lavender, blue, pink or white flowers between mid-summer and early autumn. Usually grey-green, aromatic foliage.

Paeonia suffruticosa (tree peony)
Above: Very large flowers – often 15cm (6in) across – in shades of pink or red, as well as white, in late spring. 1.5–1.8m (5–6ft).

Pyracantha (firethorn)
Small, white flowers in early summer, followed by red, orange or yellow berries. Grow against a wall or free-standing.

Syringa (lilac)
Above: *S. vulgaris* (common lilac) and other species of these popular and fragrant shrubs will all thrive on chalky soils.

BORDER PERENNIALS

Dianthus (carnations, pinks)
Above: Border carnations and pinks of all kinds will do well on chalky soils. Your garden centre should have a good selection.

Doronicum (leopard's bane)
Above: Bright yellow, single, daisy-type flowers, or doubles, in late spring and early summer. Most grow to about 60cm (2ft).

Gypsophila paniculata (baby's breath)
Masses of small white or pink flowers in summer, on a loose plant to about 1m (3ft). The lax stems benefit from a support.

Helleborus
The most popular species are *H. niger* (winter) and *H. orientalis* (spring), but there are other species and hybrids to try.

Paeonia (peony)
Above: Large single or double flowers about 12cm (5in) across, in late spring or early summer, mainly pinks and reds, 60–75cm (2–2½ft).

Scabiosa (scabious)
Above: *S. caucasica* (blue flowers from summer to autumn) is the popular border species, but other scabious will also thrive on chalk.

Verbascum (mullein)
There are several good hybrids for the border, but they tend to be short-lived. Tall spikes of pink, yellow or white flowers.

Plants for acid soil

Acid soils are generally less of a problem than alkaline ones. Most plants that tolerate a wide range of soil will do well on reasonably acid soils, especially if you add lime to neutralize the effect. The plants listed here not only thrive in acid soils but are also particularly reluctant to grow in alkaline conditions – so also use this list as an indication of what to avoid for chalky soils.

SHRUBS

Azalea
Above: There are evergreen and semi-evergreen azaleas, ranging in size from dwarfs for the rock garden to large woodland plants.

Calluna vulgaris (heather)
There are hundreds of varieties, some grown for foliage colour. Most flower late summer and autumn. 30–45cm (1–1½ft).

Camellia
Above: Large, rose-like flowers in spring, set against evergreen leaves. There are many different kinds.

Corylopsis pauciflora (winter hazel)
Spreading growth and slender branches with pale yellow catkin flowers in spring. Grows to about 1.8m (6ft).

Daboecia (Irish heath)
Above: Heather-like plant with pink or white bell-like flowers on bushy plants about 60cm (2ft) tall. Flowers from summer to autumn.

Gaultheria procumbens (winter green)
Above: A creeping plant with small evergreen leaves, useful for ground cover. Grown mainly for its red berries. 15cm (6in).

Halesia carolina (snowdrop tree)
A large, spreading shrub growing to more than 3m (10ft). Pendulous, bell-shaped white flowers appear in late spring.

Kalmia latifolia (calico bush)
Above: Evergreen with glossy green leaves and pink flowers in early summer. Grows to about 1.8m (6ft).

Pernettya mucronata
Above: An evergreen grown mainly for its berries on female plants: shades of red, pink, purple or white according to variety.

Pieris
Above: There are many good species and varieties, grown for their white flowers and red-flushed young leaves. About 1.8m (6ft).

Rhododendrons
Above: There are rhododendrons to suit all sizes of garden, and catalogues and garden centres offer hundreds of them.

Skimmia
Glossy-leaved evergreens, with red berries (if you buy a female variety or one that has flowers of both sexes). About 1m (3ft).

Ground-cover plants

Ground-cover plants will help to suppress weeds, and if used over a large area will add a sense of texture to the garden floor. Remember, however, that until they become well established, ground-cover plants are as vulnerable to dry soil and competition as most other plants.

SHRUBS

Cotoneaster dammeri
Ground-hugging shrub to about 15cm (6in). The stems root as they spread to about 1m (3ft). Red berries in autumn.

Erica carnea (heather)
Above: Most varieties make a mound of growth about 30cm (1ft) high, covered with pink, red or white flowers in winter and spring.

Euonymus fortunei (wintercreeper)
A tough evergreen about 30–45cm (12–18in) tall with a spread of 60cm (2ft) or more. Grow the bright variegated varieties.

Hedera (ivy)
Above: Both small-leaved and large-leaved types of ivy can be used for ground cover.

Hypericum calycinum
(rose of Sharon)
Above: A semi-evergreen about 30cm (1ft) tall, with large, yellow flowers and a prominent boss of stamens. A rampant spreader.

Juniperus horizontalis
(creeping juniper)
A ground-hugging conifer with a spread of 1.2m (4ft) or more. There are several good varieties varying mainly in foliage colour.

Lonicera pileata
An evergreen with horizontally spreading branches and small, bright green leaves. Grows to about 60cm (2ft) by 1.2m (4ft).

Pachysandra terminalis
Above: A low-growing ground cover about 30cm (1ft) tall, with white insignificant flowers. 'Variegata' is a more attractive plant.

Polygonum affine (knotweed)
Above: Forms a creeping mat of bright green foliage to about 15cm (6in), with small, pink, poker-like flowers. Bronze leaves in winter.

Rosa (rose)
Above: Modern ground-cover roses are very compact and ideal where you need summer colour for a sunny site.

Thymus serpyllum (creeping thyme)
Above: A ground-hugging plant with aromatic foliage and clusters of tiny, purple, white, pink or red flowers in summer.

Vinca (periwinkle)
Above: A rather untidy spreading ground cover, but useful for its usually blue flowers all summer long. There are also variegated forms.

BORDER PERENNIALS

Acaena (New Zealand burr)
Above: A colonizing carpeter with small, fern-like leaves, to about 5–8cm (2–3in) heigh. Brownish-red burrs follow summer flowers.

Ajuga reptans (bugle)
Grown primarily for foliage effect. There are purple and variegated varieties that form a carpet 5–10cm (2–4in) high.

Bergenia (elephant ears)
Above: Large, rounded, glossy green, leathery leaves. Flowers – mostly pink – in spring. 30–45cm (1–1½ft).

Cotula squalida (brass buttons)
An evergreen carpeter with fern-like foliage, growing to about 5cm (2in). Small yellow flowers appear in mid-summer.

Epimedium (barrenwort)
There are various species, grown mainly for foliage effect. Pale green leaves sometimes flushed brown or bronze. About 23cm (9in).

Geranium endressii (cranesbill)
Above: Deeply lobed foliage topped with pale pink flowers from early to late summer. Dies down in winter but summer cover is dense.

Hosta
Above: These popular foliage plants come in many variations, so choose species or varieties with leaves that particularly appeal to you.

Lamium maculatum (deadnettle)
A loose carpeter about 23cm (9in) tall. Choose a variety with silvery or attractively mottled foliage. White or purple flowers.

Lysimachia nummularia (creeping Jenny)
Top: Small, rounded leaves, yellow in 'Aurea', and yellow flowers. Needs moist soil, and only retains leaves in winter in mild areas.

Pulmonaria (lungwort)
There are many species and varieties, often with silver-splashed leaves. The spring flowers are in shades of blue and pink.

Stachys byzantina
(syn. *S. lanata*) (lamb's tongue)
Above: A grey evergreen with narrow, woolly leaves. Foliage height about 15cm (6in) but purple flower spikes grow to 45cm (18in).

Tiarella cordifolia (foamflower)
Above: A carpeter about 10cm (4in) tall with lobed, hairy leaves, topped with small spikes of white flowers in spring and early summer.

Waldsteinia ternata
Above: Evergreen about 10cm (4in) tall, spreading rapidly by creeping, rooting stems. Yellow flowers in spring and early summer.

Planting for wildlife

Wildlife will be encouraged into your garden by features such as water, bird tables and nest boxes, and plenty of borders to provide shelter and protection. But if you want to encourage bees, birds and butterflies, you also need shrubs to provide the necessary protection and plants that are rich in nectar or have a plentiful supply of berries or seeds that birds like to eat.

SHRUBS

Buddleia davidii (butterfly bush)
The flowers attract birds, butterflies, bees and many other insects.

Cotoneaster species
Above: The flowers attract insects, the berries bring the birds.

Ilex (holly)
Above: Holly berries are very attractive to birds, but be sure to plant a female variety otherwise you will not have any berries.

Lavandula (lavender)
Useful for attracting butterflies.

Leycesteria (pheasant berry)
Above: Birds love the juicy berries.

Pyracantha (firethorn)
Above: Bees and other insects are attracted to the flowers, and birds eat the berries that follow.

BORDER PLANTS

Aster (Michaelmas daisies)
Above: Butterflies, bees and other insects.

Aubrietia
Above: Butterflies, bees and other insects.

ANNUALS

Centranthus
Attracts a wide range of insects.

Erigeron (fleabane)
Butterflies, bees and other insects.

Helenium (sneezeweed)
Butterflies, bees and other insects.

Scabiosa (scabious)
Butterflies, bees and other insects.

Sedum spectabile (ice-plant)
Above: Butterflies, bees and other insects.

Solidago (golden rod)
Butterflies and insects.

Iberis (candytuft)
Above: Butterflies and other insects.

Centaurea cyanus (cornflower)
Butterflies and other insects.

Tagetes patula (French marigolds)
Above: Butterflies and other insects.

Heliotropium (heliotrope)
Butterflies and other insects.

Reseda (mignonette)
Butterflies and other insects.

Limnanthes douglasii
(poached egg flower)
Above: Butterflies and other insects.

Helianthus (sunflowers)
Birds are attracted by the seeds.

Lobularia maritima
(sweet alyssum)
Butterflies and other insects.

Dipsacus (teasel)
Birds are attracted by the seeds.

Cheiranthus (wallflower)
Butterflies and other insects.

Planting for scent

Scent adds another dimension to the garden, so plant with it in mind. Most people think first of fragrant flowers, but fragrant foliage will remain a feature for a much longer period.

SHRUBS

Chimonanthus praecox
(winter sweet)
Yellow, claw-like flowers in mid- or late winter. Needs a sheltered position and best near the shelter of a wall.

Choisya ternata
(Mexican orange blossom)
Above: Evergreen, aromatic leaves, yellow in the variety 'Sundance'. Fragrant white flowers in late spring and into summer.

Cytisus battandieri
(Moroccan broom)
Above: Small spikes of yellow flowers in summer, with strong pineapple scent. Requires a sheltered position, perhaps near a wall.

Daphne mezereum (mezereon)
Dense clusters of highly fragrant, purple-red flowers in late winter and early spring, followed by scarlet berries.

Jasminum officinale
(common jasmine)
A vigorous, twining climber with sweetly scented white flowers, pink in bud, in summer.

Lavandula (lavender)
Above: Blue, pink or white flowers between mid-summer and early autumn. Usually grey-green aromatic foliage.

Lonicera fragrantissima (shrubby honeysuckle)
A twiggy shrub with creamy-white, bell-shaped flowers in mid- and late winter. The scent is strong.

Lonicera pericylmenum
(honeysuckle)
Above: A popular, scented climber. The flowers are a combination of rose-purple and yellow. Early to late summer, depending on variety.

Philadelphus (mock orange)
Above: There are many good species and varieties, all with white, very fragrant flowers in mid- and late summer.

Rosa (rose)
Above: Roses need no introduction, but the strength of their scent varies, so consult a good catalogue if in doubt on this point.

Sarcococca (sweet box)
Clump-forming shrub with glossy, evergreen foliage and white, winter flowers that are small but very fragrant. About 1m (3ft).

Spartium junceum (Spanish broom)
Almost leafless, rush-like stems with pea-shaped, golden yellow flowers all summer. Sweet honey scent.

Syringa (lilac)
S. vulgaris (common lilac) and other species of these popular and fragrant shrubs, blooming in late spring and early summer.

Viburnum bodnantense
A winter-flowering shrub with small clusters of fragrant pink flowers on bare stems in winter.

Virburnum carlesii
Top: Sweet-scented white or pink flowers, pink in bud, in spring. Foliage usually has good autumn tints before falling.

Wisteria sinensis
Above: A very popular, large climber with cascades of sweet-scented mauve to purple-lilac flowers in late spring and early summer.

A

Acaena (New Zealand burr), 91
Acanthus spinosus (bear's breeches), 84
Acer japonicum 'Aureum', 60
Acers, 48
Achillea filipendulina (yarrow), 87
Acid soil, plants for, 89
African lily (*Agapanthus*), 84 87
Ajuga reptans (bugle), 91
Alchemilla mollis (lady's mantle), 44
Alkaline soils, 88
Anemone japonica, 86
Arbour, 67
Arches, 62
Arundo donax, 85
Aster (Michaelmas daisies), 92
Astilbe, 86
Astrantia (masterwort), 86
Aubretia, 92
Aucuba japonica (spotted laurel), 86
Azalea, 48, 89

B

Baby's breath (*Gypsophila paniculata*), 88
Bamboos, 66
Barbecue, 12, 73
Barrenwort (*Epimedium*), 91
Bear's breeches (*Acanthus spinosus*), 84
Bergenia (elephant ears), 86 91
Birdbath, 63
Bleeding heart (*Dicentra spectabilis*), 86
Blue spirea (*Caryopteris x clandonensis*), 87
Bonsai trees, 48, 49
Border pinks, 44
Borders, curved, 21, 37
Boundaries, 58, 59
disguising, 60
Box, 47
Brass buttons (*Cotula squalida*), 32, 91
Bricks, 10, 82
Broom (*Cytisus*), 87
Brunnera macrophylla, 86
Buddleia davidii (butterfly bush), 53, 88, 92
Bugle (*Ajuga reptans*), 91
Built-in furniture, 73

Butterflies, attracting, 53
Butterfly bush (*Buddleia davidii*), 53 88, 92

C

Cabbage palm (*Cordyline australis*), 32, 85
Calendula, 44
Calico bush (*Kalmia latifolia*), 89
Calluna vulgaris (heather), 89
Camellias, 48, 86, 89
Candytuft (*Iberis*), 93
Carnation (*Dianthus*), 88
Caryopteris x *clandonensis* (blue spirea), 87
Catmint (*Nepeta mussinii*), 87
Centaurea cyanus (corn flower), 93
Chalky soil, plants for, 88
Chamomile, 32
charity (*Mahonia*), 85
Cheiranthus (wallflowers), 93
Children, planning for, 42, 43
Chimonathus praecox (wintersweet), 94
Choisya ternata (Mexican orange blossom), 94
Christmas box (*Sarcococca*), 86, 94
Chusan palm (*Trachycarpus fortunei*), 85
Circles, multiple and linking, 11
circular theme, 10, 18
Cistus (rock rose), 87
Clematis, 88
Clover lawn, 33
Colour schemes, 25
Common jasmine (*Jasminum officinale*), 94
Computer, designing by, 17
Concrete paving blocks, 82
Containers, 22, 29, 40
dull corners, in, 68
grouping, 76, 77
herbs in, 55
mixed plantings, 76
upright plants in, 78
Convolvulus cneorum, 87
Cordyline australis (cabbage palm), 32, 85
Corner sites, 38, 39
Cornflower (*Centaurea cyanus*), 93
Cortaderia selloana (pampas grass), 85

Corylopsis pauciflora (winter hazel), 89
Cotoneaster, 88, 92
Cotoneaster dammeri, 90
Cottage gardens, 10, 44, 45
Cotton lavender (*Santolina chamaecyparissus*), 87
Cotula squalida (brass buttons), 32, 91
courtyard, secluded, 46, 47
Crambe cordifolia, 84
Cranesbill (*Geranium*), 87, 91
Creeping Jenny (*Lysimachia nummularia*), 91
Creeping juniper (*Juniperus horizontalis*), 90
Creeping thyme (*Thymus serpyllum*), 32, 90
Cytisus (broom), 87
Cytisus battandieri (Moroccan broom), 94

D

Daboecia (Irish heath), 89
Daphne mezereum (mezereon), 94
Deadnettle (*lamium maculatum*), 91
Design, 10,. 12, 16, 17, 18, 19, 20, 21
Diagonal theme, 18
Dianthus (carnation, pinks), 88
Dicentra spectabilis (bleeding heart), 86
Dipsacus (teasel), 93
Disguises, 66, 67
Doronicum (leopard's bane), 88
Downward slope, 34
Dull spots, 68, 69

E

Eccentric gardens, 40, 41
Echinops ritro (globe thistle), 87
Elephant ears (*Bergenia*), 86, 91

Epimedium (barrenwort), 91
Eremurus robustus (foxtail lily), 85
Erica carnea (heather), 31, 90
Erigeron (fleabane), 93
Euonymus fortunei, 90
Euphorbia (spurge), 86

F

False caster oil plant (*Fatsia japonica*), 79, 85, 86
Fences, 58
Final plan, 22
Firethorn (*Pyracantha*), 88, 92
Fleabane (*Erigeron*), 93
floodlights, 80
Flowerbeds
irregular shapes, 20
narrow, 8
Foamflower (*Tiarella cordifolia*), 91
Focal point plants, 84, 85
Focal points, 11, 62, 63
forget-me-nots, 52
Fountains, wall, 70, 71
Foxtail lily (*Eremurus robustus*), 85
French marigolds (*Tagetes patula*), 93

G

Garden furniture, 59, 72, 73
Garden illusions, 60, 61
Garden lighting, 80, 81
Garden seat, 72
Garrya elliptica (silk tassel bush), 85
Gateways, 62
Gaultheria procumbens (winter green), 89
Geranium (cranesbill), 87, 91
Globe thistle (*Echinops ritro*), 87
Golden rod (*Solidago*), 93
Grasses, 85
long, 52, 53
ornamental, 48
tough, 42
Grassless garden, 32, 33
Gravel, 22, 32, 48, 49
Ground cover, 31, 31, 90, 91
Gunnera manicata, 85
Gyposphila paniculata (baby's breath), 88

H

Halesia carolina (snowdrop

tree), 89
Hamamelis ᴠollis (witch hazel), 86
Heather (*Calluna vulgaris*), 89
Heather (*Erica carnea*), 31, 90
Hedera (ivy), 69, 90
Hedges, 58, 62
flowering shrubs, 58
shady side, 69
Helenium (sneezeweed), 93
Helianthemum nummularium (rock rose), 87, 88
Helianthus (sunflowers), 93
Heliotrope (*Heliotropium*), 93
Helleborus, 86, 88
Herb garden, 54, 55
Holly (*Ilex*), 86 92
Honeysuckle (*Lonicera pericylmenum*), 94
Hosta (plaintain lily), 86, 91
Hypericum calycinum (rose of Sharon), 90

I

Iberis (candytuft), 93
Ice-plant (*Sedum spectabile*), 93
Ilex (holly), 86, 92
Iris ensata (Japanese iris), 48
Iris *germanica*, 87
Irish heath (*Daboecia*), 89
Ivy (*Hedera*), 69, 90

J

Japanese iris (*Iris ensata*), 48
Japanese style gardens, 48, 49
Jasminum officinale (common jasmine), 94
Juniperus horizontalis (creeping juniper), 90

K

Kalmia latifolia (calico bush), 89
Kitchen garden, 56 57
Kniphofia (red hot pler), 62 85, 87
Knotweed (*Polygonum affine*), 90

L

L-shaped gardens, 38
Lady's mantle (*Alchemilla mollis*), 44
Lamb's tongue (*Stachys byzantina*), 91
Lamium maculatum (deadnettle), 91

Lavender (*Lavendula*), 88, 92 94
Leopard's bane (*Doronicum*), 88
Leycesteria (pheasant berry), 92
Lilac (*Syringa*), 88, 94
Lilyturf (*Liriope muscari*), 86
Limnanthes douglasii (poached egg flower), 93
Liriope muscari (lilyturf), 86
Lobularia maritima (sweet allysum), 93
Lonicara fragrantissima, 94
Lonicera pericylmenum (honeysuckle), 94
Lonicera pileata, 90
Love-in-a-mist (*Nigella*), 44
Lungwort (*Pulmonaria*), 86, 91
Lysimachia nummularia (creeping Jenny), 91

M

Mahonia, 86
Mahonia (Charity), 85
Masterwort (*Astrantia*), 86
Measuring, 14
Mexican orange blossom (*Choisya ternata*), 94
Mezereon (*Daphne mezereum*), 94
Michaelmas daisies (*Aster*), 92
Mignonette (*Reseda*), 93
Mock orange (*Philadelphus*), 94
Moroccan broom (*Cytisus battandieri*), 94
Mullein (*Verbascum*), 87

N

Narrow garden, 26
Nepeta mussinii (catmint), 87
New Zealand burr (*Acaena*), 91
New Zealand flax (*Phormium*), 91
Nigella (love-in-a-mist), 44

O

Ornaments, 40, 68, 74, 75
Outline, creating, 24

P

Pachysandra terminalis, 30, 31 51, 86, 90
Paeonia (poeny), 88
Paeonia suffruticosa (tree peony), 88

Pampas grass (*Cortaderia selloana*), 85
Paths, 82, 83
Patios, 28 29, 80. 81
Paulownia tomentosa, 85
Paving, 69, 82, 83
Peony (*Paeonia*), 88
Pergola, 12, 38
Periwinkle (*Vinca*), 86, 90
Pernettya mucronata, 89
Perspective 8, 9
Pheasant berry (*Leycesteria*), 92
Philadelphus (mock orange), 94
Phormium (New Zealand flax), 85
Pieris, 89
Pinks (*Dianthus*), 88
Plaintain lily (*Hosta*), 86, 91
Planning
    final plan, 22
    grids, using, 18
    measuring, 14
    paper, putting plan on, 16
    planting, for, 24, 25
    scale drawing, 16
    shape, 18
    surveying, 14
    using plan, 17
Poached egg flower (*Limnanthes douglasii*), 93
Polygonum affine (knotweed), 90
Ponds, 50
    wildlife 52
Pool, pebble, 70
Poppies, 52
Pulmonaria (lungwort) 86, 91
Pyracantha (firethorn), 88, 92

R

Raised beds, 27, 64
Rectangular theme, 10, 18
Red hot poker (*Kniphofia*), 62, 85, 87
Reseda (Mignonette), 93
Rhododendron, 86, 89
rock gardens, 35
Rock rose (*Cistus*), 87
Rock rose (*Helianthemum nummularium*), 87, 88
Rodgersia, 86
Rosa (rose), 90, 94
Rose of Sharon (*Hypericum calycinum*), 90
Rue (*Ruta graveolens*), 42

S

Sagina procumbens, 48
Sagina subulata, 48
Sandpits, 43
Santolina chamaecyparissus (cotton lavender), 87
Sarcococca (Christmas box), 86, 94
Scabious (*Scabiosa*), 88, 93
Scent, planting for, 94
Screens, 66, 67
Sedum spectabile (ice-plant), 93
Senecio, 87
Shady gardens, 64, 65
    plants for, 86
Shape, planning, 18
Sheet, planting through, 30, 31
Shrub border, ornaments in, 74
Silk tassel bush (*Garrya elliptica*), 85
Skimmia, 86, 89
Slopes, 14, 15, 34, 35
Sneezeweed (*Helenium*), 93
Snowdrop tree (*Halesia carolina*), 89
Soleirolia soleirolii, 48
Solidago (golden rod), 93
Spanish broom (*Spartium junceum*), 94
Spotlights, 80, 81
Spotted laurel (*Aucuba japonica*), 86
Spurge (*Euphorbia*), 86
Stachys byzantian (lamb's tongue), 91
Statues, 62, 63, 68, 69
    straight lines, disguising, 60
Summerhouse, 38
Sundial, 62, 63
Sunny and dry areas, plants for, 87
Surveying, 14
Sweet allysum (*Lobularia maritima*), 93
Syringa (lilac), 88, 94

T

Tagetes patula (French marigolds), 93
Teasel (*Dipsacus*), 93
Terracing, 34
Thymus serpyllum (creeping thyme), 32, 90
Tiarella cordifolia (foamflower), 91

Trachycarpus fortunei (Chusan palm), 85
Tree house, 42
Tree peony (*Paeonia suffruticosa*), 88
Tree seats, 72, 73
Triangulation, 17
Trifolium repens (white clover), 33
Trompe l'oeil, 60, 61
Tub, planting, 76

U

Upward slope, 35
Urn, planting, 76

V

Vegetables, 56, 57
Verbascum (mullein), 87, 88
Vibernum bodnantense, 94
Vibernum davidii, 86
Vinca (periwinkle), 86, 90

W

Waldsteinia ternata, 91
Wall fountains, 70, 71
Wallflowers (*Cheiranthus*), 93
Walls, low, 58
Water,
    architectural feature, as, 50
    features, 70, 71
    pebble pool, 70
    ponds, 50
    running, 50, 51
    still, 51
White clover (*Trifolium repens*), 33
Wild flowers, 52
Wildlife garden, 52, 53
Wildlife, planting for, 92, 93
Winter green (*Gaultheria procumbens*), 89
Winter hazel (*Corylopsis pauciflora*), 89
Wintersweet (*Chimonanthus praecox*), 94
Wisteria sinensis, 94
Witch hazel (*Hamamelis mollis*), 86

Y

Yarrow (*Achillea filipendulina*), 87
Yucca, 85, 87
Yucca filamentosa, 85
Yucca gloriosa, 85

Picture Acknowledgements

The Publishers gratefully acknowledge the following photographers for permission to reproduce their photographs in this book.

Jerry Harpur Garden Picture Library: 11 (bottom left), 12 (bottom right), 26, 27, 29, 41 (left), 43, 44, 47, 50, 51, 53 (left), 58 (top), 59 (top), 61 (right), 66, 67, 71 (top left), 72 (top), 77 (left) 79 (left), 81 (left, bottom right).

Peter McHoy: 1, 2, 3, 5, 7, 8, 9, 10, 11 (top left), 12 (top), 13, 15, 22, 23, 28, 30 (bottom left), 31, 32, 33, 35, 40, 41 (top right), 42, 49, 52, 53 (top right), 55 (bottom right), 58 (bottom), 59 (bottom), 61 (top left, bottom left), 62, 63 65, 69 (bottom left), 71 (top right, bottom left), 73, 75, 78, 79 (top right), 82 (left), 83, 84, 85, 86, 87, 88, 89, 90, 91, 92, 93, 94.